Remember This?

People, Things and Events
FROM **1939** TO THE **PRESENT DAY**

UK EDITION

Copyright © 2021 Say So Media Ltd.
All rights reserved.

No part of this book may be reproduced in any form or by any electronic or mechanical means including information storage and retrieval systems, without permission in writing from the publisher.

All product names and brands are property of their respective owners. No endorsement is given or implied.

With thanks for additional research by Dale Barham, Nicola Gardiner and Janice Morton.

Baby names: Office of National Statistics.

Cover images: Mary Evans - Keystone Pictures USA/zumapress.com, Gerald Wilson, Francis Frith, aviation-images.com, Tony Boxall. Cover icons from rawpixel/Freepik.

Cover Design: Fanni Williams / thehappycolourstudio.com

The Milestone Memories series including this *Remember This?* title is produced by Milestones Memories Press, a division of Say So Media Ltd.

First edition: October 2021

We've tried our best to check our facts, but mistakes can still slip through. Spotted one? We'd love to know about it: info@saysomedia.net

Rewind, Replay, Remember

What can you remember before you turned six? If you're like most of us, not much: the comforting smell of a blanket or the rough texture of a sweater, perhaps. A mental snapshot of a parent arriving home late at night. A tingle of delight or the shadow of sorrow.

But as we grow out of childhood, our autobiographical and episodic memories – they're the ones hitched to significant events such as birthdays or leaving school – are created and filed more effectively, enabling us to piece them together at a later date. And the more we revisit those memories, the less likely we are to lose the key that unlocks them.

These fragments are assembled into a more-or-less coherent account of our lives – the one we tell ourselves, our friends, our relatives. And while this one-of-a-kind biopic loses a little definition over the years, some episodes remain in glorious technicolour – although it's often the most embarrassing incidents!

But this is one movie that's never quite complete. Have you ever had a memory spring back unbidden, triggered by something seemingly unrelated? This book is an attempt to discover those forgotten scenes using the events, sounds, and faces linked to the milestones in your life.

It's time to blow off the cobwebs and see how much you can remember!

It Happened in 1939

The biggest event in the year is one that didn't make the front pages: you were born! Here are some of the national stories that people were talking about.

- HMS Courageous torpedoed off Irish coast – 519 lives lost
- Compulsory identity cards introduced for all adults and children
- First Anderson air-raid shelter built in London garden
- IRA 'bicycle' bomb blast kills five, injures 70 in Coventry
- Anglo-Saxon ship and treasures dug up at Sutton Hoo, Suffolk
- Dig for Victory campaign launched to ease food shortages
- Britain declares war on Germany after Nazis invade Poland
- Government introduces petrol rationing
- Lord Haw Haw makes first Nazi propaganda radio broadcast to UK
- Operation Pied Piper evacuates millions from cities (right)
- HMS Royal Oak sunk off Orkney Scapa Flow – 833 lives lost
- Women's Auxiliary Air Force set up to aid the RAF's war effort
- BBC launches new national radio station The Home Service
- Britain's armed services mobilised, ready for active service
- Spitfires shoot down first enemy aircraft over the UK
- Malcolm Campbell sets world water speed record in boat Blue Bird
- IRA bombs London Underground stations
- Tank and cavalry units combine to form Royal Armoured Corps
- Robert Donat and Greer Garson star in Goodbye, Mr Chips
- Government Code and Cypher School moves to Bletchley Park
- Conscription to armed forces for all able men aged 18 to 41

Born this year:
- TV broadcaster and writer David Frost born in Tenterden, Kent
- Monty Python funnyman John Cleese born in Weston-Super-Mare
- Cricketer Rachael Heyhoe Flint born in Wolverhampton

Keystone Pictures USA/ZUMAPRESS.com/Mary Evans

TO BE SHEWN.

Mothers wave goodbye to their children at Waterloo Station as Operation Pied Piper begins. Over 1.5 million children left towns and cities during the following three days – although over half were returned by early 1940, against government advice, when the threat of bombing raids appeared to be an empty one. As the war intensified, further evacuation waves followed.

On the Bookshelf When You Were Small

The books of our childhood linger long in the memory. These are the children's classics, all published in your first ten years. Do you remember the stories? What about the covers?

1940	Horton Hatches the Egg by Dr Seuss
1940	Lassie Come Home by Eric Knight
1941	Missee Lee by Arthur Ransome
1943	The Gremlins by Roald Dahl
1943	**The Little Prince by Antoine de Saint-Exupéry** In 1935, poet, aristocrat and aviator de Saint-Exupéry crash-landed in the desert. His hallucinations before eventual rescue were the seeds of the story that would later become the bestseller Le Petit Prince.
1945	Three Railway Engines by Rev W Awdry
1945	The Moomins and the Flood by Tove Jannson
1945	Pippi Longstocking by Astrid Lindgren
1945	Stuart Little by EB White
1946	Thomas the Tank Engine by Rev W Awdry
1946	First Term at Malory Towers by Enid Blyton
1947	**Goodnight Moon by Margaret Wise Brown** Margaret Wise Brown didn't have any children, and once said that she didn't especially like them, either. Nevertheless, she bequeathed all future royalties for the book to Albert, a neighbour's nine-year-old son.
1947	Billy Bunter of Greyfriars School by Frank Richards
1949	The Secret Seven by Enid Blyton
1949	Amazon Adventure by Willard Price
1949	No Boats on Bannermere by Geoffrey Trease

Around the World in Your Birth Year

Here are the events from abroad that were big enough to make news at home in the year you were born. And you won't remember any of them!

- ✦ Italian troops invade Albania; King Zog forced into exile
- ✦ Severe earthquake hits Chillan, Chile – over 30,000 dead
- ✦ Nylon stockings debut at San Francisco World Fair
- ✦ Italy-Germany Pact of Steel creates military/political alliance
- ✦ John Steinbeck's Depression novel The Grapes of Wrath published
- ✦ Russian troops invade Finland, starting 'Winter War'
- ✦ Nazis imprison Jews in squalid ghettos in occupied countries
- ✦ Siam renamed Thailand
- ✦ Franco becomes head of state of Spain's new Nationalist regime
- ✦ UK navy sinks German ship Graf Spee in first key naval battle
- ✦ Erzincan earthquake strikes eastern Turkey, killing 33,000
- ✦ US Civil War-era epic Gone With The Wind opens in cinemas
- ✦ Germany and USSR sign Molotov-Ribbentrop pact to
- ✦ partition Poland
  Spanish Civil War ends as Franco's nationalists take Madrid
- ✦ Peruvian girl becomes mother at age five
- ✦ Mahatma Gandhi 'death fast' is protest for Indian political reform
- ✦ Jewish refugee ship St Louis refused asylum by Cuba and USA
- ✦ Musical fantasy film The Wizard of Oz opens in cinemas
- ✦ US mobster Al Capone released from prison due to ill health

Born this year:
- ✧ US singer Tina Turner born Anna Mae Bullock in Nutbush, Tennessee
- ✧ Handmaid's Tale author Margaret Atwood born in Ottawa, Canada
- ✧ Feminist writer Germaine Greer born in Melbourne, Australia
- ✧ US actor and producer Harvey Keitel born in New York

Boys' Names When You Were Born

Stuck for a baby name in the early 20th century? The answer was simple: use your own. Will nobody think of the poor genealogists? Here are the most popular names in England and Wales in 1939.

John
The early 20th century belonged to John: having elbowed 19th century William out of the way, he took the top spot for nearly fifty years.

Peter
William
Brian
David
James
Michael
Ronald
Kenneth
George
Robert
Thomas
Alan
Derek
Raymond
Anthony

Rising and falling stars:
Neville made his first (and last) Top 100 appearance at number 83. Also new to the list: Malcolm, Barry, Bryan, Roger, Clive and Abdul. Names we haven't seen since: Herbert, Derrick, Ivor, Desmond, Wilfred, Sydney, Cecil, Fred, Arnold and Alec.

A note about other parts of the UK:
Baby name data isn't available until 1974 for Scotland and the turn of the century for Northern Ireland. How different are they? In the mid-seventies around a third of Scotland's Top 100 boys' names weren't in the English and Welsh equivalent – but the highest ranked of these was Gordon at number 30. By 2019, Scotland-only names ranked 4th (Harris), 7th (Lewis), 18th (Brodie), 22nd (Finlay) and more.

Girls' Names When You Were Born

Some parents pick names that are already popular. Others try to pick something more unusual – only to find out a few years later that thousands had the same idea.

Margaret
Jean
Mary
Joan
Patricia
Sheila

Sheila was one of a clutch of names that would never be more popular than they were in the late thirties and early forties. That also goes for Barbara, Doreen, June, Shirley, Audrey and Brenda.

Barbara
Doreen
June
Shirley
Dorothy
Joyce
Maureen
Elizabeth
Audrey
Brenda
Kathleen
Sylvia
Eileen
Pamela
Betty
Beryl
Ann
Irene

Rising and falling stars:

Shirley burst into the Top 100 in 10th place; others also making their first showing included Valerie, Norma and Judith. Marina came in at 35 and was never seen again. Also on the way out: Olive, Winifred, Thelma, Gladys and Enid.

Things People Did When You Were Growing Up...

...that hardly anyone does now. Some of these we remember fondly; others are best left in the past!

- Use a mangle
- Do your National Service (it ended in 1960)
- **Use an outside toilet**
  Slum clearances and grants saw the end of most outside toilets, although in 2010 around 40,000 properties still had one.

- Take the trolley bus to school
- Fetch coal from the cellar
- Wear a hat to work
- **Use a coal tar vaporizer**
  A coal tar inhaler or vaporizer – probably made by Wright's, with the matching liquid – seemed like a good idea for treating whooping cough. It wasn't. A 1930s example held by the National Trust has a simple caption: 'This is poisonous.'

- Travel without a seatbelt
- **Rent a TV**
  When tellies cost a fortune (and frequently broke), renting a TV made sense. Where to go? Radio Rentals, who promised, 'You'll be glued to our sets, not stuck with them!'

- **Wear a housecoat**
  Who can think of a housecoat and curlers without remembering Coronation Street's Hilda Ogden?

- Scrub your doorstep
- Creosote the fence (banned for DIY in 2003)
- **Smoke a pipe**
  Stephen Fry was the last Pipe Smoker of the Year, in 2003.
- **Spank (or be spanked)**
  Corporal punishment ended in most schools in 1986. It is illegal in Scottish and Welsh homes, but not in England or N. Ireland.

- Pay the Pools collector
- Build a soapcart
- **Write a letter**
  Royal Mail still handles 10 billion letters each year but very few are handwritten. More than a fifth of UK children have never received a letter.

Old-fashioned Games

In a pre-digital age, boardgames ruled. Many of these predate you buy decades, centuries or more but still played; others gather dust in attics and charity shops.

1928	Escalado
1934	Sorry!
1935	**Monopoly**

The origins of this stalwart lie with The Landlord's Game, an education tool patented in 1904 by Elizabeth Magie. (The anti-monopoly version – Prosperity – didn't catch on.) It was the first game to feature a never-ending path rather than a fixed start and finish.

1938	Buccaneer
1938	Scrabble
1935	Whot!
1947	Subbuteo
1949	**Cluedo**

Cluedo, or Clue as it is known in the USA, introduced us to a host of shady country house characters and a selection of murder weapons. For years those included a piece of genuine lead pipe – thankfully replaced on health grounds.

1925	Dover Patrol
1851	**Happy Families**

The original and much-copied Happy Families card game was launched for the Great Exhibition in 1851. For 20th Century children, Happy Families also means the million-selling book series by Allan Ahlberg, based loosely on the card game, which in turn inspired a BBC series.

1889	**Tiddlywinks**

Trademarked as Tiddledy-Winks by Joseph Fincher, this much-maligned game has nevertheless found fans at elite universities, spawned countless spin-offs and rule variations (known in Tiddlywink parlance as 'perversions').

1896	Ludo
1892	Chinese Chequers
1938	Totopoly
Ancient Egypt	Mancala

Things People Do Now...

...that were virtually unknown when you were young.
How many of these habits are part of your routine or even
second nature these days? Do you remember the first time?

- Shop on Sunday (made possible in England and Wales in 1994)
- Microwave a curry
- **Leave a voicemail**
  At least you'll never have to change the cassette again!
- **Watch last night's TV**
  Nowadays, you don't have to remember to set the VCR (and get a
  small child to help you do it). BBC iPlayer was the UK's first
  on-demand, streaming service, launched in 2007.

- Strim grass
- Change a fitted sheet
- Recharge your toothbrush
- Order a takeaway meal... to be delivered
- Delete a photo
- **Fit a disposable nappy**
  The first disposable 'napkins' went on sale in 1949 as two-part
  Paddis, invented by Valerie Hunter Gordon.

- Eat an avocado
- Use Google
- Take a shower
- **Make a video call (right)**
- Buy a cheap flight
- **Floss your teeth**
  Not a flosser? Take heart from a 2016 US research review:
  evidence for its benefit is very weak, and official advice to floss
  was dropped. Poking around with those pesky interdental
  brushes is how you should be spending your time (and money).

- Pressure wash your patio
- **Stick a self-adhesive stamp**
  You can probably still remember the taste of stamp glue, even
  though the sticky versions were introduced in 1993.

- Answer an email (or send it to spam)
- **Use a duvet**
  Sir Terence Conran is credited with finally persuading Brits to
  ditch the blankets when he introduced duvets in his Habitat
  stores in the sixties.

Mary Evans / Everett Collection

Zoom, Skype, FaceTime and more: if you weren't making face-to-face calls before the lockdowns of 2020, that's probably when you made your first. But it has taken 50 years to catch on and for technology to catch up: shown above is AT&T's PicturePhone, demonstrated in 1964 at New York's World's Fair. (The cost didn't help: renting a pair of devices for three minutes cost the equivalent of £100.)

Popular Food in the 1950s

Few would wish the return of fifties food, even the dishes introduced after rationing finally ended in 1954. Tinned food, stacked high. For flavour, take your pick: ketchup, brown sauce, or salad cream. Keep your olive oil in the bathroom cabinet. But a few favourites live on: who can resist a coronation chicken sandwich?

Milkshakes
Thick, creamy and an ideal hiding place for a lethal dose of poison. That's what the CIA thought when they plotted to slip a pill into Castro's beloved chocolate milkshake. Fortunately for the Cuban leader, the pill stuck to the freezer door.

Chop Suey

Real cream cakes

Bananas
In the 1950s, Gros Michel bananas – the dominant banana sold – were wiped out by the Panama disease, nearly destroying the banana industry.

Peaches

Frosties
Introduced in 1954 as Sugar Frosted Flakes, this new cereal was an instant hit – as was Tony the Tiger.

Frozen chicken

Tinned pineapple
Think pineapple, think Hawaii. Pineapples are still cultivated there, although the state's last cannery closed in 2006.

Spam fritters
Dubbed the 'Miracle Meat' when it was introduced in the late thirties, Spam is no longer made in the UK but it's still popular. Worldwide, around 7 billion cans have been sold; 44,000 cans are still produced every hour.

Baked Alaska

Devilled eggs

Coronation chicken

Hamburgers
In the US during WWII, hamburgers were briefly rebranded 'liberty steaks' in a renewed bout of food-as-propaganda. In World War I, sauerkraut was 'liberty cabbage' while French fries became 'freedom fries' during the Iraq war.

Pre-war Chocolate

Many of the chocolate bars we enjoy today were dreamed up long before WWII – though recipes, sizes and names have mostly been given a tweak or two over the decades to keep them as our newsagent favourites.

1800s	**Fry's Chocolate Cream** The first chocolate bars to be mass-produced.
1905	Cadbury Dairy Milk
1908	Bourneville
1914	Fry's Turkish Delight
1920	Flake
1926	Cadbury's Fruit & Nut
1927	**Jaffa Cake** Her Majesty's Customs and Excise tried to argue that a Jaffa Cake is a biscuit and subject to VAT. McVitie's won the day, in part because Jaffa cakes go hard when stale, unlike biscuits which go soft.
1929	Crunchie
1932	**Mars Bar** Want to buy a Mars bar in the US? Ask for a Milky Way.
1932	Penguin
1935	Aero
1935	**Milky Way** The Milky Way is not named after our galaxy, but instead after a type of malted milk, or milkshake as it's now known.
1936	Milky Bar
1937	**Kit Kat** Before Joseph Rowntree trademarked the term 'Kit Kat' in 1911 and the snack's eventual launch in the thirties, the name was most commonly associated with a mutton pie made by pastry chef Christopher Catt. He served it in his London Kit-Cat Club during the late 17th Century.
1937	Rolo
1939	**Marathon** In 1990, Marathon became Snickers: the US name since its 1930 launch (named after Frank Mars's horse). In the seventies, Mars sold a chocolate bar in the US called the Marathon – and it's still on sale here as the Curly Wurly.

Cars of the 1950s

Do you remember your first road trip? Bare legs welded to the hot plastic seats, buffeted by gusts of warm air through the open windows and not a seatbelt to be seen. There's a fair chance you'll have been cooped up in one of these fifties favourites.

Austin Westminster

Ford Prefect
In The Hitchhiker's Guide to the Galaxy, an arriving alien picks the name Ford Prefect thinking it would be inconspicuous.

Vauxhall Velox

Sunbeam Talbot

Rover 60

Ford Anglia
Features on the cover of Harry Potter and the Chamber of Secrets.

Ford Consul

Hillman Minx

Morris Minor
Originally named Mosquito, the name was changed at the last minute as it was feared that the name would deter conservative buyers. It went on to become the first million-selling British car.

MG Magnette

Morris Oxford

Singer Gazelle

Standard Vanguard
Named after a Navy battleship to appeal to ex-servicemen.

Austin Cambridge

Wolseley / Riley One Point Five
The Riley One Point Five and the Wolseley shared features including the engine, suspension and dimensions. The Riley was originally intended as a replacement for the Morris Minor.

Ford Popular

Land Rover
The first Land Rover was inspired by World War II jeeps, with the steering wheel in the middle. A Land Rover with tank tracks for agricultural work and a monster truck version followed.

Austin A30
Dubbed the steel teddy bear due to its rounded, cute appearance.

Keystone Press Agency/Keystone USA via ZUMAPRESS.com/Mary Evans

1958 brought a rather less welcome motoring innovation: the parking meter. The first meters installed in Mayfair, London (sixpence for an hour, a shilling for two), triggered the predictable result from day one: parked cars crammed onto neighbouring streets without restrictions, below.

Fashion in the Fifties

Your transition into adulthood and the discovery of your own style began in the fifties, amid a new age of Hollywood glitz. But how many of these newly fashionable designers and outfits could be found in your wardrobe?

Petticoat
Winklepicker
Inspired by medieval footwear, winklepickers were named after the pointed pin used to eat winkles. Also known as 'mosquito chasers' in Sweden and Norway, and 'roach stompers' in some parts of the US.

Norman Hartnell
Twinset
Designed by Otto Weisz in the 1930s for Pringle of Scotland, the twinset's popularity soared when it was taken up as work wear and worn by Grace Kelly, Audrey Hepburn and Jackie Kennedy.

Nylon
Flatties
Seamless stockings
Victor Stiebel
Waspie corsets
Kitten heels
Christian Dior
Dior was criticised for using so much material in his designs, and King George VI reportedly forbade Princesses Elizabeth and Margaret from wearing the designs while rationing was in place.

Tweed sports jacket
Cat-eye glasses
Pencil skirt
Hardy Amies
Brothel creepers
Bikini
Unveiled in 1946 by Louis Réard and named after Bikini Atoll, a US nuclear test site. Louis Réard couldn't find a fashion model who would wear the design, so he hired a nude dancer instead.

Grace Kelly
In 1956, Grace Kelly wore one of the most famous wedding dresses of all time. The Hermès bag she carried was renamed in her honour: the Kelly bag.

Household Goods in 1947

In 1947, the government calculated inflation for the first time using a basket of frequently purchased goods. This list has been reviewed ever since; the changes mirror our ever-changing tastes and habits. Here's what housewives were buying when you were small.

Wireless licence

Sugar lumps
Sugar lumps were patented in 1843 by Jakub Kryštof Rad. Sugar was previously sold in a solid block called a sugarloaf, cautiously cut into pieces with a tool called sugar nippers.

Swedes
A 'food of last resort', swedes were also used as a filler in fruit jams.

Table mangle

Currants
Currants are dried, black seedless grapes from the Greek island of Zante (and nothing to do with fresh, tart red or black currants).

Prunes

Compound cooking fat

Condensed milk

Custard powder

Plum jam

Tram fare

Gabardine raincoat
Gabardine was originally waterproofed using lanolin (the grease secreted by sheep). It was invented by Thomas Burberry in 1879, patented in 1888 and worn by Mallory and Irvine on their Everest expedition of 1924.

Tweed sports coat

Bib and brace overall

Rayon blouse
Rayon was produced as a cheap alternative to silk. Although made from natural cellulose, the manufacturing process uses highly toxic chemicals.

Smocked frock

Gramophone record

Lamp oil

Winceyette gown

On the Silver Screen When You Were 11

From family favourites to the films you weren't allowed to watch, these are the movies that drew the praise and crowds when you turned 11.

Night and the City 🎞 Richard Widmark, Gene Tierney
Orpheus 🎞 Jean Marais, François Périer
Treasure Island 🎞 Bobby Driscoll, Robert Newton
Cyrano de Bergerac 🎞 José Ferrer, Mala Powers
Father of the Bride 🎞 Spencer Tracy, Joan Bennett
Gone to Earth 🎞 Jennifer Jones, David Farrar
Sunset Boulevard 🎞 William Holden, Gloria Swanson
The line 'All right, Mr DeMille, I'm ready for my close-up' was voted #7 on AFI's list of greatest movie quotes.

The Elusive Pimpernel 🎞 David Niven, Edmond Audran
So Long at the Fair 🎞 Jean Simmons, Dirk Bogarde
King Solomon's Mines 🎞 Deborah Kerr, Stewart Granger
The Blue Lamp 🎞 Jack Warner, Jimmy Hanley
Odette 🎞 Anna Neagle, Trevor Howard
Stage Fright 🎞 Jane Wyman, Marlene Dietrich
Alfred Hitchcock gave Dietrich unprecedented control over the way her scenes were shot, lauding her versatility on set.

Annie Get Your Gun 🎞 Betty Hutton, Howard Keel
Born Yesterday 🎞 Judy Holliday, William Holden
Morning Departure 🎞 John Mills, Richard Attenborough
In a Lonely Place 🎞 Humphrey Bogart, Gloria Grahame
All About Eve 🎞 Bette Davis, Anne Baxter
All About Eve holds the record for the most female acting nominations at the Academy Awards (four).

The Asphalt Jungle 🎞 Sterling Hayden, Louis Calhern
The Wooden Horse 🎞 Leo Genn, David Tomlinson
The Men 🎞 Marlon Brando, Teresa Wright
The Men features the first on-screen performance by the incomparable Brando.

Harvey 🎞 James Stewart, Josephine Hull
Seven Days to Noon 🎞 Barry Jones, André Morell
Cinderella 🎞 Ilene Woods, James MacDonald

Comics When You Were Small

Did you spend your childhood hopping from one foot to the other, longing for the next edition of your favourite comic to appear on the shelves? If so, these may be the titles you were waiting for.

Comic Cuts ✸ (1890-1953)
Illustrated Chips ✸ (1890-1953)
The Champion ✸ (1922-1955)
The Hotspur ✸ (1933-1959)
The first-ever issues of the Hotspur were sold with a free black mask. The same mask was rebranded as the Whoopee Mask when it was given away with the Beano debut five years later.

Knockout ✸ (1939-1963)
Knockout Comics (or Knock-Out as they were originally known) ran for 24 years before merging into Valiant. However, the title was revived in 1971 (and the hyphen removed). Unlike most comics of the early 70s, every page was in colour.

Girl ✸ (1951-1964)
Boys Own ✸ (1879-1967)
The Eagle ✸ (1950-1969)
TV Comic ✸ (1951-1984)
The Topper ✸ (1953-1990)
The Dandy ✸ (1937-2012)
Beano ✸ (1938-present)
The most valuable copies of the first issue of Beano fetch over £17,000 at auction. There are only 20 left in the world today.

Around the UK

10

Double digits at last: you're old enough to eavesdrop on adults and scan the headlines. These may be some of the earliest national news stories you remember.

✦ Scot John Boyd-Orr wins Nobel Peace Prize for nutrition research
✦ Astronomer Fred Hoyle coins 'Big Bang' for creation of universe
✦ Scottish mother of six patents UK's first disposable nappy
✦ WWII clothes rationing ends
✦ Government devalues pound by 30% against US dollar
✦ Midlands transmitter brings BBC TV to viewers beyond South East
✦ Legal aid introduced to support 'equal access to justice'
✦ Cwmbran designated Wales' first new town
✦ The Republic of Ireland officially recognised by UK government
✦ Longleat becomes first stately home to open to paying visitors
✦ BBC radio's Book At Bedtime kicks off with John Buchan novel
✦ Man United's Old Trafford stadium rebuilt after WWII bombing
✦ Dockers strike – troops brought in to unload cargo
✦ First self-service coin-operated laundrette opens in London
✦ Wolverhampton Wanderers win FA cup for the third time
✦ First British passenger jet De Havilland Comet takes to sky
✦ George Orwell's dystopian novel 1984 published
✦ Peacetime National Service starts for fit males aged 17 to 21
✦ Enid Blyton's first Noddy book published
✦ John Haigh, the 'Acid Bath Murderer', found guilty and hanged by Albert Pierrepoint
✦ 'Little Kinsey' national survey on sexual behaviour begins in UK

Born this year:
⚛ Iconic 1960s model Twiggy born Lesley Hornby in London
⚛ English fast bowler Bob Willis born in Sunderland
⚛ Garden guru and author Alan Titchmarsh born in Ilkley, Yorkshire

UK Buildings

Some were loathed then, loved now; others, the reverse. Some broke new architectural ground, others helped to power a nation or entertain. All of them were built before you were 40.

1942	**Walthamstow Town Hall** The recently completed building served as a British Restaurant during the war, feeding those in need.
1942	**Wythenshawe Bus Garage** Grade II listed on account of its huge concrete arches and shell – just two inches thick. It's now used as a car park.
1951	**Royal Festival Hall** Following the bombing of the Queen's Hall during the Blitz, London was left without a major concert hall. The foundation stone was laid by PM Clement Attlee in 1949.
1961	**Dungeness Lighthouse** When you build a nuclear power station that blocks out the view of a lighthouse, what do you do? Build another one.
1962	Coventry Cathedral
1963	Bankside Power Station
1964	**Post Office Tower** The tower was previously a designated secret under the Official Secrets Act and didn't appear on any OS maps. It was a pretty prominent secret, though, and was used as a filming location for TV and film during this time.
1966	Centre Point
1966	**Severn Bridge** Grade I listed, and since 2018, free to cross (both ways!).
1967	Queen Elizabeth Hall
1976	**National Exhibition Centre (NEC)** The NEC was originally planned for Leicester but the council rejected the plan, fearing it would be a flop. The current centre was opened by the Queen and it has been home to Crufts since 1991.

Household Goods in 1952

Five years on and rationing is still in place, goods are still scarce and war-time staples such as corned beef are still on the menu. Change is on the horizon though, with imported goods increasingly popular and radio sets bought alongside gramophone records.

Wild rabbit
Consumption of wild rabbit peaked in the early 1950s. Wild rabbit was easily sourced and could be used instead of chicken.

Ox liver
Imported lamb
The UK has been importing lamb from New Zealand since the 1800s. And yet we export lamb, too: the UK demands higher-end cuts of meat while exporting low value cuts.

Sild
Imported butter
Rationing of butter lasted until 1954 and when it ended, the British doubled their butter consumption.

Turnips
Pipe tobacco
Pipe tobacco remained in the basket of goods until the 1950s.

Distemper
Omnibus fares
Electric fire
Electric iron
Hard soap
Scrubbing brush
Electric light bulb
By the start of World War II, two thirds of homes were connected to the National Grid; lights were the first use of electricity in most homes.

Domestic help
Girls' gym tunic
Infant nursery squares
Radio set
Trolley bus fares

Female Wimbledon Winners

Aged 15 in 1887, Lottie Dod was the youngest to win Wimbledon. Aged 37 in 1908, Charlotte Cooper Sterry was the oldest. These are the winners when you too were still in with a (slim) chance! Men, PTO!

1952-54	Maureen Connolly
1955	Louise Brough
1956	Shirley Fry
1957-58	**Althea Gibson**

Gibson was a prodigiously talented, trail-blazing athlete – the first black tennis player to successfully fight for her right to play at the elite level. She won eleven Grand Slam tournaments. She could commentate, sing, play the saxophone and later played golf at the highest level.

1959-60	Maria Bueno
1961	Angela Mortimer
1962	Věra Suková
1963	Margaret Smith
1964	**Maria Bueno**

Bueno caused controversy by wearing a white dress with a pink underskirt, drawing grasps from the crowd.

1965	Margaret Smith
1966-68	**Billie Jean King**

King lobbied for equal pay, won the Battle of the Sexes against Bobby Riggs and was the first woman to be chosen as Sports Illustrated's Sportsperson of the Year.

1969	Ann Jones
1970	Margaret Court
1971	Evonne Goolagong
1972-73	Billie Jean King
1974	Chris Evert
1975	Billie Jean King
1976	Chris Evert

Wimbledon: The Men

In the men's tournament, Becker won at the tender age of 17. At the top end, Federer won in 2017 at the age of 35. But in 1909, in the amateur era, Arthur Gore was a nimble 41 years young – giving us our 'winning window' of 17 to 41.

1956-57	Lew Hoad
1958	Ashley Cooper
1959	**Alex Olmedo**

After retiring, Alex Olmedo taught tennis for many years at The Beverly Hills Hotel. Students included Katharine Hepburn, Robert Duvall, Chevy Chase, Charlton Heston, and Jon Lovitz.

1960	Neale Fraser
1961-62	Rod Laver
1963	**Chuck McKinley**

McKinley had a habit of yelling 'Oh, Charley, you missed that one!' after a bad shot. He was suspended for four months for throwing his racket into the stands and retired from tennis at the age of 24.

1964-65	Roy Emerson
1966	Manuel Santana
1967	John Newcombe
1968-69	Rod Laver
1970-71	John Newcombe
1972	**Stan Smith**

Outside tennis, Stan Smith is best known for his best-selling line of Adidas sports shoes.

1973	Jan Kodeš
1974	Jimmy Connors
1975	**Arthur Ashe**

Ashe contracted HIV from a blood transfusion following a heart operation, and worked to raise the awareness of HIV and AIDS before his death at the age of 49. The Arthur Ashe Stadium in New York was named in his memory.

1976-80	Björn Borg

Books of the Decade

Ten years that took you from kids' adventure books to dense works of profundity - or maybe just grown-up adventures! How many did you read when they were first published?

1949	**Nineteen Eighty Four by George Orwell** An early title for the book was The Last Man in Europe. It is commonly believed that Orwell chose the year as an inversion of 1948, the year he wrote the book.
1949	The Sheltering Sky by Paul Bowles
1951	Foundation by Isaac Asimov
1951	The Day of the Triffids by John Wyndham
1952	The Old Man and the Sea by Ernest Hemingway
1952	East of Eden by John Steinbeck
1953	**Fahrenheit 451 by Ray Bradbury** Fahrenheit 451 contains technology we'd recognise today including flat screen TVs, video calling, and earbuds. How far ahead was Bradbury thinking? We can't know, as it's never stated.
1953	Go Tell it on the Mountain by James Baldwin
1953	Casino Royale by Ian Fleming
1953	The Go-Between by L P Hartley
1954	The Lord of the Rings by JRR Tolkien
1954	**Lord of the Flies by William Golding** Rejected several times before publication, sold poorly on release and one of the most-banned books in the USA. In 1983, Golding won the Nobel Prize in Literature for novels that 'illuminate the human condition.'
1954	Lucky Jim by Kingsley Amis
1954	Under the Net by Iris Murdoch
1955	Lolita by Vladimir Nabokov
1955	The Talented Mr. Ripley by Patricia Highsmith
1955	The Quiet American by Graham Greene
1956	Diamonds Are Forever by Ian Fleming
1957	**On the Road by Jack Kerouac** Kerouac typed On the Road on a single sheet of paper that was 120 feet long. The original ending is missing - because a cocker spaniel ate it.

Around the UK

Here's a round-up of the most newsworthy events from across the country in the year you turned (sweet) 16.

- ✦ Operation Snowdrop airdrops supplies to snow-stranded villages
- ✦ BBC monopoly broken as ITV makes first broadcast
- ✦ Murderer Ruth Ellis is last woman hanged in UK
- ✦ Churchill, 80, resigns as prime minister due to ill-health
- ✦ Kenneth Kendall becomes first BBC newsreader seen on screen
- ✦ Birds-Eye fish fingers appear on British plates
- ✦ McWhirter twins compile first Guinness Book of Records
- ✦ Anthony Eden succeeds Churchill as prime minister (right)
- ✦ Airfix launches its first plastic model plane kit
- ✦ English-language version of Waiting for Godot opens in London
- ✦ Kim Philby cleared of being 'Third Man' in Cambridge spy ring
- ✦ UK claims uninhabited island of Rockall in North Atlantic
- ✦ Aircraft carrier HMS Ark Royal enters active service
- ✦ Cardiff becomes official capital of Wales
- ✦ Stirling Moss becomes first Briton to win British Grand Prix
- ✦ Hugh Gaitskell succeeds Clement Attlee as Labour Party leader
- ✦ Engineer Christopher Cockerel patents hovercraft design
- ✦ First TV advert appears on ITV for Gibbs SR toothpaste
- ✦ Salk polio vaccine trialled across UK
- ✦ Princess Margaret cancels wedding to Group Captain Townsend
- ✦ Heatwave and drought hits UK

Born this year:
- ꝏ Journalist and TV presenter Kirsty Wark born in Dumfries
- ꝏ World Wide Web inventor Tim Berners-Lee born in London
- ꝏ Conductor Simon Rattle born in Liverpool

Keystone Pictures USA/ZUMAPRESS.com/Mary Evans

It was the 'dullest postwar election', proclaimed the BBC. Anthony Eden, recently appointed PM after the resignation of his wife's uncle (Winston Churchill), won by a landslide across the United Kingdom. Although telegenic, Eden campaigned traditionally (above) and couldn't rely on this newly popular medium: the '14-day rule' hampered broadcasters' ability to cover political issues and campaign coverage was still sparse.

TV Newsreaders: The Early Days

Trusted, familiar, and mostly with received pronunciation: these are the faces that brought you and your family the news, and the dates they shuffled their papers.

Richard Baker 📺 (1954-82)
In 1954, Baker introduced the BBC's first TV news broadcast. Seventies children know his voice as the narrator of Mary, Mungo and Midge.

Robert Dougall 📺 (1955-73)
Kenneth Kendall 📺 (1955-69)
Angela Rippon 📺 (1975-2002)
The UK's first regular female newsreader and known nationwide for her 1976 Morecambe and Wise appearance.

Jill Dando 📺 (1988-99)
The shocking murder of Dando on her doorstep in 1999 remains unsolved.

Moira Stuart 📺 (1981-2007)
Peter Woods 📺 (1964-81)
Woods is the biological father of BBC journalist and presenter Justin Webb.

Nan Winton 📺 (1960-61)
Winton was the BBC's first on-screen female newsreader in a shortlived 1960 trial deemed unacceptable by viewers.

Reginald Bosanquet 📺 (1967-79)
Michael Aspel 📺 (1960-68)
Corbet Woodall 📺 (1963-67)
Anna Ford 📺 (1976-2006)
Jan Leeming 📺 (1980-87)
Lynette Lithgow 📺 (1988-96)
Selina Scott 📺 (1980-86)
Sue Lawley 📺 (1981-88)
Alongside her news duties, Lawley is best known for her 18-year stint presenting BBC Four's Desert Island Discs. She left the role in 2006.

Julia Somerville 📺 (1983-99)

Fifties TV Gameshows

Gameshows got off to a rocky start in the UK, but the advent of commercial TV in 1955 – and ad-funded prizes – boosted the format into primetime, where it has remained ever since. Many of these early shows have since been remade, but how many of the originals do you remember?

Tell the Truth

Twenty Questions
Host Gilbert Harding, dubbed by the BBC as Britain's 'best-loved and best-hated man', was particularly drunk during one recording. He insulted two of the panellists, caused chaos by failing to recognise an answer, and ended the show early. Read more about Harding on page 36.

What's My Line?
Arguably the nation's first TV gameshow, first on screens in 1951.

Round Britain Quiz
Top of the Form
Twenty-One
Beat the Clock
Concentration
Crackerjack
Do You Trust Your Wife?

Double Your Money
In 1959, Sir Bobby Charlton appeared as a contestant on the show and won the top prize of £1,000, answering questions on pop music. Dame Maggie Smith also appeared as a hostess for a short time before her acting career took off.

Name That Tune
Opportunity Knocks
Spot the Tune

Take Your Pick!
Take Your Pick! was the first gameshow to be broadcast on commercial TV, debuting on the newly launched ITV in 1955. The income generated by adverts made it the first UK gameshow to give away cash prizes.

Two for the Money
Keep it in the Family
Make Up Your Mind

Stamps When You Were Young

Stamp collecting was the first serious hobby for many 20th century children. Commemorative issues weren't issued until the twenties, but soon became highly collectible – and the perfect gift for uncles in need of inspiration. These stamps may well have started your collection.

1924-5	**British Empire Exhibition** Designed to showcase Britain's strengths in an era of declining global influence, the exhibition left a legacy: the Empire Stadium (later renamed Wembley Stadium). The stamps were the UK's first commemorative issue, sixty years after the USA did the same.
1929	**9th Universal Postal Union Congress, London** Arguably of little interest to few outside philatelic circles, this was the first of several self-referential issues over successive decades. See also the Inter-Parliamentary stamps first issued in 1957.
1935	George V Silver Jubilee
1937	George VI Coronation
1940	**Centenary of the first adhesive postage stamp** Everyone has heard of the first adhesive stamp, issued in 1840: the Penny Black. (Perforations didn't come along until the 1854 Penny Red.) The glue on commemorative stamps contained around 14 calories!
1946	Victory
1948	Royal Silver Wedding
1948	Olympic Games
1949	The 75th Anniversary of the Universal Postal Union
1951	Festival of Britain
1951	George VI (high value 'definitives')
1953	The coronation of Queen Elizabeth II
1955	Castles (high value 'definitives')
1957	**World Scout Jamboree** Held in Sutton Coldfield; 50,000 Scouts attended. After heavy rain, the US Air Force was called in to help.
1957	46th Inter-Parliamentary Union Conference
1958	6th British Empire and Commonwealth Games

The Biggest Hits When You Were 16

The songs that topped the charts when you turned 16 might not be in your top 10 these days, but you'll probably remember them!

Mambo Italiano ♪ Rosemary Clooney
The Finger of Suspicion ♪ Dickie Valentine
Softly, Softly ♪ Ruby Murray
Give Me Your Word ♪ Tennessee Ernie Ford
Stranger in Paradise ♪ Tony Bennett
Before Tony Bennett made this song popular, it first featured in the musical Kismet.

Unchained Melody ♪ Jimmy Young
There have been more than 1,500 recordings of Unchained Melody since it was written in 1955 and it is one of only two songs to hit number one four times (the other is Do They Know It's Christmas).

Dreamboat ♪ Alma Cogan
Rose Marie ♪ Slim Whitman
The Man from Laramie ♪ Jimmy Young
As well as hitting the top of the charts as a performer – including a number one with one of those 1,500 versions mentioned above – Jimmy Young spent three decades as a beloved DJ on BBC Radio 2.

Hernando's Hideaway ♪ Johnston Brothers
Rock Around the Clock ♪ Bill Haley and the Comets
Rock Around the Clock was the first UK single to sell over one million copies.

Christmas Alphabet ♪ Dickie Valentine

Household Goods in 1956

Dance halls and designer goods, holidays and hobbies: a nation that's 'never had it so good', according to Harold Macmillan's famous 1957 speech. Here are the most notable purchases in the nation's 1956 shopping basket.

Youth club admission

Crispbread

Pope's eye steak

Luncheon meat

Rice

NHS prescription

The controversial one shilling charge was introduced in 1952, prompting NHS founder Aneurin Bevan to resign. Prime Minister Harold Wilson abolished the prescription charge in 1965, before reintroducing it in 1968, with some exemptions.

Meat extracts

Plastic emulsion paint

TV tube replacement

Electric lamp

Cardigan

Tweed sports coat

Corset

Impractical corsets took a dive in popularity during the first half of the 20th century but experienced a resurgence during the 1950s when Christian Dior's 'new look' became fashionable.

Cat food

Smocked frock

Motor insurance

Driving test fee

In 1956, the driving test fee doubled to £1 before being suspended due to the Suez crisis. In 1957, three-year driving licences were introduced (and lasted until licenses were extended in 1976).

Dance hall admission

By 1953, dance halls were second in only to cinema. Around 70% of couples at the time are said to have met on the dance floor.

Camera film

Telegram

Blockbuster Movies When You Were 16

These are the movies that everyone was talking about. How many of them did you see (or have you seen since)?

The Colditz Story John Mills, Eric Portman
Oklahoma! Gordon MacRae, Gloria Grahame
The director chose to use as little camera movement as possible to give Oklahoma! a true Broadway feel.

Raising a Riot Kenneth More, Shelagh Fraser
One Good Turn Norman Wisdom, Joan Rice
I Am a Camera Laurence Harvey, Julie Harris
Above Us the Waves John Mills, John Gregson
The Dam Busters Richard Todd, Michael Redgrave
The Cockleshell Heroes Trevor Howard, Anthony Newley
The Seven Year Itch Marilyn Monroe, Tom Ewell
Doctor at Sea Dirk Bogarde, Brigitte Bardot
To Catch a Thief Cary Grant, Grace Kelly
Grant came out of retirement to star in this movie for Alfred Hitchcock.

Guys and Dolls Marlon Brando, Jean Simmons
Lady and the Tramp Larry Roberts, Barbara Luddy
The Rose Tattoo Anna Magnani, Burt Lancaster
The Ladykillers Alec Guinness, Peter Sellers
Rebel without a Cause James Dean, Natalie Wood
Director Nicholas Ray made the supporting cast get into real fights as part of their audition.

Richard III Laurence Olivier, Ralph Richardson
The Quatermass Xperiment Brian Donlevy, Jack Warner
Summertime Katharine Hepburn, Rossano Brazzi
You Lucky People! Tommy Trinder, Mary Parker
East of Eden James Dean, Raymond Massey
This was the first of only three films in Dean's often-discussed career.

The End of the Affair Deborah Kerr, Van Johnson
The Ship That Died of Shame George Baker, Richard Attenborough
Marty Ernest Borgnine, Betsy Blair

Gameshow Hosts of the Fifties and Sixties

Many of these men were semi-permanent fixtures, their voices and catchphrases almost as familiar as our family's. Some were full-time entertainers, born to the stage; others seemed rather less suited to the spotlight!

Ted Ray... ⋈ (Joker's Wild)
and his son, Robin Ray ⋈ (Face the Music)
Peter Wheeler ⋈ (Crossword on Two, Call My Bluff)
Robert Robinson ⋈ (Brain of Britain, Ask the Family)
McDonald Hobley ⋈ (Come Dancing, It's a Knockout)
David Jacobs ⋈ (Juke Box Jury)
Shaw Taylor ⋈ (Password, Pencil and Paper)
Eamonn Andrews ⋈ (Crackerjack!)
Roy Plomley ⋈ (Many a Slip)
Gilbert Harding ⋈ (Twenty Questions, What's My Line?)
Harding was a teacher and policeman before working in radio and television. Resentful of his fame, Harding was once left mortified on the London Underground when he was recognised by fellow passengers who failed to notice that TS Eliot was also in the same carriage.

Bamber Gascoigne ⋈ (University Challenge)
Tommy Trinder ⋈ (Sunday Night at the Palladium)
Bruce Forsyth ⋈ (Beat the Clock)
Bruce Forsyth first appeared on television in 1939. He had many talents including playing the ukulele and accordion, singing, dancing and acting. In his later years, Forsyth stated that he regretted presenting so many gameshows.

Leslie Crowther ⋈ (Billy Cotton Band Show, Crackerjack)
Bob Monkhouse ⋈ (The Golden Shot)
While serving in the RAF, Bob Monkhouse drafted a letter to the BBC from his group captain, stating that 18-year-old Monkhouse was a war hero and deserved an audition. His group captain signed the letter without reading it; Monkhouse got his audition.

Hughie Green ⋈ (Opportunity Knocks)
Derek Batey ⋈ (Mr and Mrs)
Wilfred Pickles ⋈ (radio show Have a Go)

Kitchen Inventions

The 20th-century kitchen was a playground for food scientists and engineers with new labour-saving devices and culinary shortcuts launched every year. Here are some your parents – and now you – wouldn't be without.

1929	**Dishwasher** The first hand-operated dishwasher was created in 1885 by inventor and socialite, Josephine Cochrane, who was tired of her servants chipping her fine china. In 1929, Miele brought out an electric, top-loading model. Front-loading and drying functions followed in 1940; automation in 1960.
1937	Blender
1939	Pressure cooker
1940	Chest freezer
1945	**Fridge** If you think today's American-style fridges are big, consider the Large Hadron Collider in Geneva. With a circumference of 17 miles and 9,300 magnets, it's chilled to -270C before use. That would definitely keep your milk cold.
1948	Kenwood mixer
1955	Automatic kettle
1956	**Non-stick pan** You can thank a French angler's wife for your non-stick pans: it was she who noticed her husband's habit of coating his gear in non-stick Teflon, and suggested he did the same to her pans. Scrambled egg fans owe her a life-long debt.
1960	**Tupperware** In 1960, Tupperware parties arrived in the UK. Earl Tupper's 1948 invention took off when a US single mother called Brownie Wise started home sales and the social selling concept proved equally successful here. This icon of female entrepreneurship was dismissed in 1958 for being too outspoken.
1974	Microwave
1974	Food processor
1976	**Deep fat fryer** The Egyptians, Romans and Greeks were all known to have been keen on deep frying their food – often items that look uncommonly like today's doughnuts (minus the jam).

Around the World When You Turned 18

These are the headlines from around the globe as you were catapulted into adulthood.

✦ New York's serial 'Mad Bomber' arrested after 16-year hunt
✦ First programming language Fortran developed by US IBM team
✦ Ghana celebrates independence from British rule
✦ US toy company produces first flying disc the Frisbee
✦ Tunisia abolishes monarchy to become republic
✦ Ruthless dictator 'Papa Doc' Duvalier elected as Haiti's president
✦ Passenger jet Boeing 707 makes first flight in USA
✦ Elvis drafted for National Service in US army
✦ Treaty of Rome establishes European Economic Community
✦ US rocker Jerry Lee Lewis marries 13-year-old cousin
✦ Soviets launch world's first satellite Sputnik I
✦ Dr Seuss' children's book The Cat in the Hat is instant hit
✦ Leonard Bernstein's musical West Side Story debuts on Broadway
✦ International Atomic Energy Agency set up
✦ Suez Canal reopens to international shipping
✦ Asian flu pandemic causes up to two million deaths
✦ US army escorts black pupils to enrol in white Little Rock school
✦ USSR sends first animal Laika the dog into space on Sputnik 2

Born this year:
ॐ US pop star and teen idol Donnie Osmond born in Ogden, Utah
ॐ Champion golfer Seve Ballesteros born in Pedreña, Spain
ॐ Cuban-American singer Gloria Estefan born in Havana
ॐ US director Shelton Jackson 'Spike' Lee born in Atlanta, Georgia

FA Cup Winners Since You Were Born

Many fans have waited decades to see their team lift the cup; many more are still waiting. Here are the teams that have hoisted the trophy in your lifetime (last win in brackets).

Derby County ⚽ (1945-46)
Charlton Athletic ⚽ (1946-47)

Charlton Atheltic played in the 1946 and 1947 FA Cup Finals. In both games, the ball inexplicably burst. It hasn't happened since.

Blackpool ⚽ (1952-53)
Newcastle United ⚽ (1954-55)
Aston Villa ⚽ (1956-57)

After Aston Villa won the final in 1895, the FA Cup was stolen from a shop window display in Birmingham. The thief confessed 63 years later, stating he had melted the trophy down to make coins.

Bolton Wanderers ⚽ (1957-58)
Nottingham Forest ⚽ (1958-59)
Wolverhampton Wanderers ⚽ (1959-60)
West Bromwich Albion ⚽ (1967-68)
Leeds United ⚽ (1971-72)
Sunderland ⚽ (1972-73)
Southampton ⚽ (1975-76)
Ipswich Town ⚽ (1977-78)
West Ham United ⚽ (1979-80)
Coventry City ⚽ (1986-87)
Wimbledon ⚽ (1987-88)
Tottenham Hotspur ⚽ (1990-91)
Everton ⚽ (1994-95)
Liverpool ⚽ (2005-06)
Portsmouth ⚽ (2007-08)
Wigan Athletic ⚽ (2012-13)
Manchester United ⚽ (2015-16)
Chelsea ⚽ (2017-18)
Manchester City ⚽ (2018-19)
Arsenal ⚽ (2019-20)
Leicester City ⚽ (2020-21)

Around the UK

Voting. Placing a bet. Buying a legal drink. Turning 18 is serious stuff. Here's what everyone was reading about in the year you reached this milestone.

✦ Prime minister Sir Anthony Eden resigns after Suez crisis
✦ Harold MacMillan succeeds Eden as prime minister
✦ Britain tests first hydrogen bomb over Maiden Island in Pacific
✦ Harold Macmillan makes 'never had it so good' speech
✦ Jodrell Bank Observatory opens in Cheshire
✦ Asian flu pandemic reaches UK; vaccine made available
✦ Star winger Stanley Matthews plays final England game aged 42
✦ BBC ends 6pm transmission break aka 'Toddlers' Truce'
✦ Flying boat crash on Isle of Wight kills 45 (right)
✦ Windscale fire spews radioactive dust across UK and Europe
✦ Birthplace of The Beatles, the Cavern Club opens in Liverpool
✦ Astronomy series The Sky at Night airs, hosted by Patrick Moore
✦ Consumer advice magazine Which? first published
✦ BBC's Panorama dupes many with April Fool spaghetti tree hoax
✦ Petrol rationing following Suez crisis ends
✦ First premium bond winners selected by ERNIE machine
✦ Norwich becomes first UK city council to install a computer
✦ Duke of Edinburgh is made prince of the realm
✦ UK government grants independence to Singapore
✦ Scottish biochemist Alexander Todd wins Nobel Chemistry Prize
✦ Award-winning film The Bridge on the River Kwai hits UK cinemas

Born this year:
❧ Film and method actor Daniel Day-Lewis born in Kensington, London
❧ Political singer-songwriter Billy Bragg born in Barking, Essex
❧ Gold-medal winning ice skater Jayne Torvill born in Nottingham

Keystone Pictures USA/ZUMAPRESS.com/Mary Evans

The Aquila Airways flying boat was in the air for just eight minutes before making the distress call back to Southampton: Engine 4 had failed. At some point on its return to the airport, Engine 3 also failed for reasons that were never established. With no power on one side, the plane crashed into a quarry. Despite the efforts of nearby soldiers, 45 crew and passengers died, making it the second worst air crash in the UK at the time.

Medical Advances Before You Were 21

A girl born in the UK in 1921 had a life expectancy of 59.6 years (boys: 55.6). By 2011 that was up to 82.8 (79 for boys), thanks to medical advances including many of these.

1940	Metallic hip replacement
1941	**Penicillin**

Years after his discovery of penicillin, Alexander Fleming was given a tour of a modern, sterile lab. His guide said, 'Think of the wonders you would have discovered with a lab like this.' He replied, 'Not penicillin.'

1942	Mechlorethamine chemotherapy
1943	Kidney dialysis
1944	Disposable catheter
1944	**Asperger syndrome described**

Named after Hans Asperger, the Austrian paediatrician who led the research into the condition. Asperger described his patients as 'little professors'.

1947	Defibrillation
1956	Paracetamol
1949	Intraocular lens (myopia and cataracts)
1950	Polio vaccine
1951	Munchausen syndrome (described)
1952	**Artificial heart**

The first artificial heart was built by General Motors. Before the operation, the patient saw two dogs with shaved chests running around, and discovered that they had been the final test subjects. The patient survived the procedure too.

1952	Cloning
1953	Ultrasound
1956	**Metered-dose inhaler**

The daughter of head of Riker Laboratories asked why her asthma medicine couldn't be in a can like hair spray instead of traditional glass squeeze bulb containers.

1958	Pacemaker
1959	Bone marrow transplant

Popular Girls' Names

If you started a family at a young age, these are the names you're most likely to have chosen. And even if you didn't pick them, a lot of British parents did!

Susan
After thirty years, Susan takes the top spot from Margaret.

Linda
Christine
Margaret
Janet
Patricia
Carol
Elizabeth
Mary
Anne
Ann
Jane
Jacqueline
Barbara
Sandra
Gillian
Pauline
Elaine
Lesley
Angela
Pamela
Helen
Jennifer
Valerie

Jean
Slides from the Top 100 are usually gentle. But not for Jean: by the sixties, she was gone.

Catherine

Rising and falling stars:
A quarter of names in this Top 100 haven't been seen since, including Rita, Geraldine and Doreen. Taking their place are names such as Gail, Dawn, Anna, Fiona and Beverley.

Animals Extinct in Your Lifetime

Billions of passenger pigeons once flew the US skies. By 1914, they had been trapped to extinction. Not every species dies at our hands, but it's a sobering roll-call. (Date is year last known alive or declared extinct).

1939	Toolache wallaby, Australia
1940	Javan lapwing, Indonesia
1943	Desert bandicoot, Australia
1945	Wake Island rail, Wake Pacific atoll
1949	Sinú parakeet, Colombia
1951	Yemen gazelle
1952	**Deepwater cisco fish** The deepwater cisco, once found in two Michigan lakes, was overfished and crowded out by invasive parasites and herring. Result? Extinction.
1952	San Benedicto rock wren, Mexico
1962	Red-bellied opossum, Argentina
1963	Kākāwahie honeycreeper, Hawaii
1964	South Island snipe, New Zealand
1966	Arabian ostrich
1967	**Yellow blossom pearly mussel, USA** Habitat loss and pollution proved terminal for this resident of Tennessee.
1968	Mariana fruit bat (Guam)
1971	Lake Pedder earthworm, Tasmania
1972	Bushwren, New Zealand
1979	Yunnan Lake newt, China
1981	Southern gastric-brooding frog, Australia
1986	Las Vegas dace
1989	Golden toad (see right)
2000	**Pyrenean ibex, Iberia** For a few minutes in 2003 this species was brought back to life through cloning, but sadly the newborn ibex died.
2001	Caspian tiger, Central Asia
2008	Saudi gazelle
2012	**Pinta giant tortoise** The rarest creature in the world for the latter half of his 100-year life, Lonesome George lived out his days in the Galapagos as the last remaining Pinta tortoise

The observed history of the golden toad is brief and tragic. It wasn't discovered until 1964, abundant in a pristine area of Costa Rica. By 1989 it had gone, a victim of rising temperatures.

Popular Boys' Names

Here are the top boys' names for this year. In many instances it's merely a reshuffle of the popular names from the previous decade; but in the lower reaches, change is afoot...

David
David has wrestled control of the top spot from John, and he'll keep it for twenty years.

John
Stephen
Michael
Peter
Robert
Paul
Alan
Christopher
Richard
Anthony
Andrew
Ian
James
William
Philip
Brian
Keith
Graham
Kevin
Martin
Colin

Steven
Steven powers in at number 23 and will stay in the Top 100 for the rest of the century.

Thomas
Kenneth

Rising and falling stars:
Farewell Bernard, Frank, Norman, Leonard, Lawrence and Clifford. Give a big Top 100 welcome to Jeremy, Julian and all the G's: Gerard, Garry, Gareth and Gregory and Glenn.

Popular Movies When You Were 21

The biggest stars in the biggest movies: these are the films the nation was enjoying as you entered adulthood.

La Dolce Vita 🎬 Marcello Mastroianni, Anita Ekberg
Peeping Tom 🎬 Carl Boehm, Anna Massey
Peeping Tom suffered a major audience backlash due to the subject matter and was pulled five days after release.

Spartacus 🎬 Kirk Douglas, Laurence Olivier
Stanley Kubrick told cinematographer, Russell Metty, to take a seat and let him do all the work behind the camera. Metty ended up winning his only Oscar for the film.

Inherit the Wind 🎬 Spencer Tracy, Fredric March
The Millionairess 🎬 Sophia Loren, Peter Sellers
The Sundowners 🎬 Deborah Kerr, Robert Mitchum
The Alamo 🎬 John Wayne, Richard Widmark
BUtterfield 8 🎬 Elizabeth Taylor, Laurence Harvey
Breathless 🎬 Jean-Paul Belmondo, Jean Seberg
Kidnapped 🎬 Peter Finch, James MacArthur
Ocean's Eleven 🎬 Frank Sinatra, Dean Martin
Sons and Lovers 🎬 Trevor Howard, Dean Stockwell
Psycho 🎬 Anthony Perkins, Janet Leigh
The famous shower scene contains 70 edits in just 45 seconds, making it one of the most studied montages in cinema history.

The League of Gentlemen 🎬 Jack Hawkins, Nigel Patrick
School for Scoundrels 🎬 Ian Carmichael and Terry-Thomas
The Entertainer 🎬 Laurence Olivier, Brenda de Banzie
Carry On Constable 🎬 Sidney James, Kenneth Williams
The Magnificent Seven 🎬 Yul Brynner, Steve McQueen
The Apartment 🎬 Jack Lemmon, Shirley MacLaine
Village of the Damned 🎬 George Sanders, Barbara Shelley
The blonde wigs were custom-made with a built-in dome to make the children's craniums look bigger than usual.

The Angry Silence 🎬 Richard Attenborough, Pier Angeli
Sink the Bismarck 🎬 Kenneth More, Dana Wynter
The Trials of Oscar Wilde 🎬 Peter Finch, Yvonne Mitchell

Around the UK

A selection of national headlines from the year you turned 21. But how many can you remember?

✦ UK's first nuclear submarine HMS Dreadnought launched
✦ Bluebell Railway steam heritage line opens in Sussex
✦ First episode of Coronation Street broadcast live
✦ Princess Margaret marries photographer Antony Armstrong-Jones
✦ Macmillan's 'Winds of Change' speech points to end of empire
✦ First Ten Tors teams take on Dartmoor teenage challenge
✦ UK's first traffic wardens patrol central London (right)
✦ Lady Chatterley's Lover on sale after 32-year ban
✦ British rule in Nigeria comes to an end
✦ Britain becomes founder member of European Free Trade Assoc.
✦ UK's first successful kidney transplant undertaken
✦ Dr Martens functional yet fashionable AirWair boots go on sale
✦ Cyprus breaks free of British rule
✦ Grand National broadcast live on TV for first time
✦ Last man called up for National Service as conscription ends
✦ Sheerness naval dockyard closes – thousands of jobs lost
✦ Lionel Bart's musical Oliver! opens in London's West End
✦ Northern drama Saturday Night and Sunday Morning hits cinemas
✦ Worldwide dance craze The Twist gets Britons on the dancefloor
✦ ITV broadcasts first live league football match
✦ The Queen's second son Andrew Albert Christian Edward born

Born this year:
⚬ Cross-dressing ceramicist Grayson Perry born in Chelmsford
⚬ Gold-medal sprinter Linford Christie born in Jamaica
⚬ TV chef and food writer Nigella Lawson born in London
⚬ British actress Tilda born Katherine Matilda Swinton in London

Keystone Pictures USA/ZUMAPRESS.com/Mary Evans

In September 1960, a new team of 40 officers with yellow-banded caps hit the streets of London. The days of carefree parking were over; parking tickets were here to stay. Traffic Warden GW Crowe kicks off his ticketing career above with a Bentley, but the first ticket ever given was to Dr Thomas Creighton who had parked his Ford Popular at a jaunty angle outside a hotel to attend to a call-out. A predictable public outcry

The Biggest Hits When You Were 21

The artists you love at 21 are with you for life. How many of these hits from this milestone year can you still hum or sing in the bath?

Starry Eyed ♪ Michael Holliday
Why ♪ Anthony Newley
Poor Me ♪ Adam Faith
Running Bear ♪ Johnny Preston
My Old Man's a Dustman ♪ Lonnie Donegan
A rugby-inspired version of this song was released in New Zealand, changing the title to My Old Man's an All-Black.

Cathy's Clown ♪ The Everly Brothers
Three Steps to Heaven ♪ Eddie Cochran
Three Steps to Heaven was a posthumous number one for Eddie Cochran, topping the charts two months after his death in a Bristol taxi crash.

Please Don't Tease ♪ Cliff Richard
Apache ♪ The Shadows
John Lennon once said that Cliff Richards and the Shadows were the only thing worth listening to before The Beatles came along.

Tell Laura I Love Her ♪ Ricky Valance
Only the Lonely ♪ Roy Orbison
Bruce Springsteen references Only the Lonely in his 1975 masterpiece, Thunder Road.

It's Now or Never ♪ Elvis Presley
I Love You ♪ Cliff Richard

Popular Food in the 1960s

Convenient ready meals, 'fancy foreign food'… the sixties menu had it all. The chemists joined the dinner party, too, with additives and processes that made our new favourites easy and cheap to produce. We'd take a while to work out if this was always such a good idea!

Vesta curry or Chow Mein

Lager
'Lager' comes from the German word 'lagern', meaning 'to store', as lager takes longer to produce than other ales.

Coco Pops

Fish fingers
The largest fish finger ever made was 6ft long and weighed 136 kg. No word on whether the chef dipped it in ketchup.

Spaghetti Bolognese
You shouldn't include oregano, basil or garlic in the 'ragu' (not bolognese). And for goodness' sake, use tagliatelle, not spaghetti. Or… accept that it is as inauthentic as the Vesta curry and enjoy, like millions of Brits learned to do in the sixties.

Chicken Tikka Masala

Cheese and onion crisps
The first flavoured crisps were created by Joe 'Spud' Murphy (founder of Irish brand Taytos) in the late 1950s.

Crêpe Suzette

Chicken liver pâté

Angel Delight
Angel Delight doubled the dessert market when it was invented in 1967. Wallace and Gromit gave it another push in 1999.

Fray Bentos pies

Instant coffee

Frozen vegetables
Clarence Birdseye was the first person to freeze food for mass production, having got the idea from an Inuit in 1912.

Swedish meatballs

White bread
A new Chorleywood process introduced enzymes and additives and high-speed mixing. The result? Soft, cheap bread that sticks to the roof of your mouth. A nation couldn't get enough of it.

Fashion in the Sixties

However extravagant your taste in clothing, it's a dead cert that you could find something to shock and impress in the sixties. But whether you were old or bold enough to carry off a pair of bell bottoms or a paper dress is a secret that should remain between you and your photo albums!

Shift dresses
Mini skirt
Popularised by Mary Quant who named the skirt after her favourite car - although not everyone was a fan. Coco Chanel described the skirt as 'just awful', and it was banned in some European countries.

Five-point cut
Vidal Sassoon
Sassoon had a temper. He would give clients a slap of a comb if they touched their hair while he was cutting it.

John Bates
Biba
Biba started as a mail order business, advertising a pink gingham dress in the Daily Mirror. 17,000 orders were placed and a shop was opened. On its opening day, the store sold out of its only product line.

St Michael American Tan tights
Dr Scholl
Orlon, Crimplene, Terylene, Spandex, PVC and Vinyl
Paper dresses
Twiggy
Jackie Kennedy
In 1962, Jackie Kennedy wore a leopard print coat which caused a spike in demand for leopard skin, leading to the death of up to 250,000 leopards. The coat's designer, Oleg Cassini, felt guilty about it for the rest of his life.

Little black dress
First introduced by Coco Chanel in the 1920s, the little black dress received a fifties update from Christian Dior. Audrey Hepburn's LBD sold for £467,200 in 2006.

Jean Shrimpton
Jane Birkin

Around the World When You Turned 25

By your mid-twenties, TV coverage of news in far-flung places brought global stories into our homes almost as fast as they happened. How many do you remember?

✦ Japanese bullet train service opens for Tokyo Olympics
✦ Beatlemania hits USA as Fab Four make first visit
✦ The Rolling Stones release self-titled debut album
✦ US Civil Rights Act passed to end segregation and discrimination
✦ Ford unveils new model Mustang at New York World Fair
✦ US civil rights leader Martin Luther King given Nobel Peace Prize
✦ Sidney Poitier is first black American to win Best Actor Oscar
✦ Tokyo hosts first Summer Olympics held in Asia
✦ Lyndon B Johnson elected US president in landslide victory
✦ 57 East Germans escape to West via Berlin Wall tunnel
✦ US pilot Jerrie Mock is first woman to fly solo around the globe
✦ Boxer Cassius Clay aka Muhammad Ali wins world heavyweight title
✦ Tanganyika and Zanzibar unite to form Tanzania
✦ US boosts military presence in Vietnam after Tonkin Gulf attack
✦ Anti-apartheid leader Nelson Mandela jailed for life
✦ UN sends 7,000 troops to calm Greek-Turkish Cypriot civil war
✦ Soviet premier Kruschev ousted and succeeded by Brezhnev
✦ President Kaunda takes power as Zambia becomes independent
✦ Palestinian Liberation Organisation established
✦ UK film stars Elizabeth Taylor and Richard Burton marry

Born this year:
✧ US funk-rocker Leonard Albert 'Lenny' Kravitz born in New York
✧ Australian actor Russell Crowe born in Wellington, New Zealand
✧ French actress Juliette Binoche born in Paris
✧ Former US First Lady Michelle Obama born in Chicago, Illinois

Cars of the 1960s

For every much-loved Hillman Imp or trusted Vauxhall Victor, the sixties boasts a glamorous Aston Martin DB5 or a covetable Jaguar E-type. Has any decade delivered for the motoring public like the sixties?

Mini
Famously featured in the 1969 film The Italian Job, Mini manufacturer BMC didn't want the car used in the film and refused to donate any. However, the director insisted that British cars should be used in a British film and over a dozen were used.

Triumph Herald

Vauxhall Victor
The design of the Vauxhall Victor was based on the style of American cars, which didn't appeal to everyone's taste in 1960s Britain. The car also gained a negative reputation for rusting.

Austin 1100

Sunbeam Tiger

Aston Martin DB5
The Aston Martin DB5 has been described as the most famous car in the world, following its 1964 debut in Goldfinger. In 1968, the car used by James Bond in the film was stripped of the weapons and gadgets and resold as a used car. It was stolen in 1997 and is rumoured to be in the Middle East.

Hillman Hunter

Lotus Elan
The Lotus Elan was designed by Ron Hickman, who subsequently left Lotus and went on to design the Black & Decker Workmate. Early versions of the Elan were also available as a kit that could be assembled by the buyer.

Ford Cortina
The Ford Cortina was launched in 1962 and later proved to be the best-selling car of the 1970s in its Mk3 guise. Designed as a new version of the Ford Consul, the name was changed to Cortina after the Italian ski resort Cortina d'Ampezzo, host to the 1956 Winter Olympics.

Rover 3500

MGB

Vauxhall HA Viva

Books of the Decade

Were you a voracious bookworm in your twenties? Or a more reluctant reader, only drawn by the biggest titles of the day? Here are the new titles that fought for your attention.

1959	The Tin Drum by Günter Grass
1959	The Naked Lunch by William S Burroughs
1959	Cider with Rosie by Laurie Lee
1960	**To Kill a Mockingbird by Harper Lee**

The story was turned down by several publishers. Lee was so frustrated that she threw it out of her apartment window. She doubted that the book would have any success, but it continues to sell a million copies a year.

1961	**Catch-22 by Joseph Heller**

The book was originally titled Catch-18 but was changed due to its similarity to the title of the novel Mila 18, which had just been announced.

1961	A House for Mr. Biswas by V S Naipaul
1962	**A Clockwork Orange by Anthony Burgess**

Burgess was diagnosed with a brain tumour and wrote five novels in a year to provide his wife with income. It turned out to be a misdiagnosis; he lived for another 30 years.

1962	The Golden Notebook by Doris Lessing
1963	Cat's Cradle by Kurt Vonnegut
1963	V by Thomas Pynchon
1964	Herzog by Saul Bellow
1964	Last Exit to Brooklyn by Hubert Selby
1965	Dune by Frank Herbert
1966	Wide Sargasso Sea by Jean Rhys
1966	The Jewel In The Crown by Paul Scott
1967	One Hundred Years of Solitude by Gabriel Garcia Marquez
1967	The Outsiders by SE Hinton
1967	Poor Cow by Nell Dunn
1968	2001: A Space Odyssey by Arthur C Clarke

Stamps in the Sixties

The UK hit its stride with commemorative stamps in the sixties. There were dry centenary and congress issues, but in 1965 the Postmaster General, Tony Benn, removed the need to include a large monarch portrait. The result? The kind of stamps every young collector would want.

1963	Freedom From Hunger
1963	Lifeboat Conference
1963	Red Cross Centenary Congress
1964	Opening of the Forth Road Bridge
1965	Winston Churchill Commemoration
1965	700th anniversary of Parliament
1965	Centenary of the Salvation Army
1965	**Antiseptic Surgery Centenary** Celebrates the introduction of surgical sterilisation by Joseph Lister.
1965	Commonwealth Arts Festival
1965	25th Anniversary of the Battle of Britain
1965	Opening of the Post Office Tower
1966	Westminster Abbey
1966	Landscapes
1966	**1966 World Cup** Stamps to mark England's role as hosts were hastily reissued in August 1966 with ENGLAND WINNERS added.
1966	British birds
1966	British technology
1966	900th anniversary of the Battle of Hastings
1966	**Christmas** The first UK Christmas stamps. The idea was championed by Tony Benn and the stamps designed by two 6-year-olds – winners of a Blue Peter competition.
1967	British wild flowers
1967	British paintings
1967	British discoveries and inventions
1967	Sir Francis Chichester's solo circumnavigation
1968	British bridges
1969	Concorde's first flight

Sixties TV Gameshows

Gameshows in the sixties were dominated by a few stalwarts, though a few short-lived experimental formats and US adaptions were tried. Without any serious competition, audiences were enormous. How many do you remember watching with your family?

Call My Bluff
Almost every episode from the first eight series of Call My Bluff has been wiped from the BBC archives. There were 263 episodes in series one to eight, and only seven episodes still survive.

Face the Music

Just a Minute

Ask the Family

University Challenge
Several celebrities appeared on University Challenge before they became famous. These include Stephen Fry, David Starkey, Sebastian Faulks, Julian Fellowes, and Miriam Margolyes (who swore when she answered a question incorrectly). University Challenge has a claim to be the longest running TV quiz show, alongside A Question of Sport.

For Love or Money

Mr and Mrs
After watching the Canadian version of Mr and Mrs, Derek Batey was inspired to develop a UK version of the show for Border Television. Batey hosted over 500 episodes, as well as 5,000 on stage after developing a theatrical version.

Play Your Hunch

Take Your Pick

Brain of Britain

Double Your Money
A November 1966 episode drew the nation's highest gameshow audience of nearly 20 million viewers.

Exit! It's the Way-Out Show

Many a Slip

Three Little Words

Crossword on 2

Around the UK

Another decade passes and you're well into adulthood. Were you reading the news, or making it? Here are the national stories that dominated the front pages.

✦ Ocean liner Queen Elizabeth 2 makes maiden voyage to New York
✦ British troops deployed in Northern Ireland in response to riots
✦ Death penalty for murder abolished
✦ Robin Knox-Johnston first to sail solo non-stop around globe
✦ Pre-decimal halfpenny coins phased out
✦ John Lennon weds Japanese artist Yoko Ono in Gibraltar
✦ Aussie media mogul Rupert Murdoch takes over News of the World
✦ Oarsman John Fairfax first to row solo across Atlantic
✦ Victoria Line opens on London Underground
✦ Charles, Prince of Wales, receives title in Caernarfon
✦ John Lennon returns MBE over UK complicity in Vietnam and Biafra
✦ Cult toy Space Hopper bounces into the shops
✦ The Beatles give last public performance on Apple Records roof
✦ Surreal sketch show Monty Python's Flying Circus airs on BBC1
✦ Ulster unionist Rev. Ian Paisley jailed over illegal protest
✦ Kray Twins Reggie and Ronnie sentenced to life for double murder
✦ Concorde makes first test flight at twice the speed of sound (right)
✦ Regular colour TV broadcasts begin on BBC1 and ITV
✦ Gibraltar's border with Spain closed by General Franco
✦ Lionel Bart's Dickensian musical Oliver! wins six Oscars
✦ Quirky kids' series The Clangers first broadcast on BBC1

Born this year:
🐭 12 Years A Slave director Steve McQueen born in London
🐭 Award-winning actress Catherine Zeta-Jones born in Swansea
🐭 Fashion designer Alexander McQueen born in London

The Royal Aeronautical Society (National Aerospace Library) / Mary Evans Picture Library; aviation-images.com / Mary Evans Picture Library

Concorde made its first scheduled flight in 1976, but seven years earlier the first prototypes left the hangar: Concorde 001 (made in France), and Concorde 002, made in Bristol. Chief test pilot Brian Tubshaw (top left) is seen above preparing for its maiden flight on 9 April alongside co-pilot John Cochrane.

Concorde's livery changed several times over its lifetime but was only certified when predominantly white to keep the temperature down at supersonic speeds. There was one exception: in 1996, Pepsi paid to paint one aircraft blue as part of its $500m rebrand. The paint job carried a speed restriction.

The Biggest Hits When You Were 30

How many of these big tunes from the year you turned thirty will still strike a chord decades later?

Ob-La-Di, Ob-La-Da ♪ Marmalade
Ob-La-Di, Ob-La-Da was originally recorded by The Beatles and written by Paul McCartney – but not released in the UK or America. Its first live performance by any of The Beatles was in 2009.

Lily the Pink ♪ The Scaffold
Albatross ♪ Fleetwood Mac
Albatross – an instrumental – is the only Fleetwood Mac song to reach number one on the UK charts.

Blackberry Way ♪ The Move
Where Do You Go To ♪ Peter Sarstedt
Peter Sarstedt's elder brother Richard also had a number one hit in the UK with Well I Ask You in 1961 – performed under the moniker of Eden Kane.

I Heard It Through the Grapevine ♪ Marvin Gaye
Israelites ♪ Desmond Dekker & The Aces
Get Back ♪ The Beatles with Billy Preston
Dizzy ♪ Tommy Roe
Comedian Vic Reeves joined forces with the Wonder Stuff to release a cover of Dizzy in 1991. Both versions went to number one in the UK.

Honky Tonk Women ♪ The Rolling Stones
Je t'aime... moi non plus ♪ Jane Birkin
Sugar, Sugar ♪ The Archies

...and the Movies You Saw That Year, Too

From award winners to crowd pleasers, here are the movies that played as your third decade drew to a close.

Sweet Charity 🎬 Shirley MacLaine, John McMartin
Till Death Do Us Part 🎬 Warren Mitchell, Dandy Nichols
Play Dirty 🎬 Michael Caine, Nigel Davenport
A Touch of Love 🎬 Ian McKellen, Sandy Dennis
The Italian Job 🎬 Michael Caine, Benny Hill
Caine did not have a driver's license when he took on the film. He learned to drive while on-set (you never see him driving).

Mosquito Squadron 🎬 David McCallum, Suzanne Neve
Paint Your Wagon 🎬 Lee Marvin, Clint Eastwood
The Virgin Soldiers 🎬 Lynn Redgrave, Hywel Bennett
The Wild Bunch 🎬 William Holden, Ernest Borgnine
Easy Rider 🎬 Peter Fonda, Dennis Hopper
In the scene where Jack Nicholson tries marijuana for the first time and talks about UFOs, the actors really did get stoned.

The Gypsy Moths 🎬 Burt Lancaster, Deborah Kerr
Three Into Two Won't Go 🎬 Rod Steiger, Claire Bloom
Mackenna's Gold 🎬 Gregory Peck, Omar Sharif
Women in Love 🎬 Alan Bates, Oliver Reed
True Grit 🎬 John Wayne, Kim Darby
Despite being one of the most recognisable Western stars of all time, this is the only film for which Wayne won an Oscar.

Midnight Cowboy 🎬 Dustin Hoffman, Jon Voight
Voight told the studio he would do this film for nothing. They took that offer literally, only paying him $14 for his meals.

Kes 🎬 David Bradley, Lynne Perrie
Hannibal Brooks 🎬 Oliver Reed, Michael J Pollard
Battle of Britain 🎬 Christopher Plummer, Michael Caine
The Assassination Bureau 🎬 Oliver Reed, Diana Rigg
Age of Consent 🎬 James Mason, Helen Mirren
Cactus Flower 🎬 Walter Matthau, Ingrid Bergman
Oh! What a Lovely War 🎬 Laurence Olivier, John Gielgud
Hamlet 🎬 Nicol Williamson, Anthony Hopkins

Around the House

Sometimes with a fanfare but often by stealth, inventions and innovations transformed the 20th-century household. Here's what arrived between the ages of 10 and 30.

1950	Fairy Liquid
1951	Video tape recorders
1953	Marker pens
1955	**TV remote control**

A wired remote control called Lazy Bones made its debut in 1950, at the behest of an advert-loathing electronics company president. But in 1956 the future arrived: a wireless version called Space Command.

1956	Flat pack furniture
1957	Electric watches
1958	Pledge furniture polish
1959	The dimmer switch
1961	Cordless power drills
1962	**Satellite television**

Despite being invented in 1962, satellite television did not reach UK shores until 1990 when British Satellite Broadcasting was launched. Later that year, it merged with Sky to become BSkyB.

1963	Push button telephones
1963	**Lava lamps**

Edward Craven Walker invented the lava lamp after seeing a homemade egg timer in a Dorset pub. The egg timer consisted of wax and water inside a cocktail shaker type contraption. The shaker was placed in the water with a boiling egg. When the wax melted, the egg was ready.

1964	Flat screen and portable TVs
1965	**AstroTurf**

AstroTurf was originally called ChemGrass, and invented by chemicals giant Monsanto. It was rebranded in 1966.

1965	Cordless phones
1965	Plastic chairs and plastic wheelie bins
1969	Bean bags

British Prime Ministers in Your Lifetime

These are the occupants of 10 Downing Street, London, during your lifetime, not including Larry the resident cat. Don't be deceived by that unassuming, black, blast-proof door: Number 10 features a warren of more than 100 rooms.

1937–40	Neville Chamberlain
1940–45	Winston Churchill
1945–51	Clement Attlee
1951–55	Sir Winston Churchill
1955–57	Sir Anthony Eden
1957–63	**Harold Macmillan**

Macmillan was the scion of a wealthy publishing family, but the biggest secret of his life was kept under wraps: his wife Dorothy's 30-year affair with fellow Conservative (and Krays associate) Robert Boothby. Macmillan died aged 92; his last words were, 'I think I will go to sleep now.'

1963–64	Sir Alec Douglas-Home
1964–70	Harold Wilson
1970–74	Edward Heath
1974–76	Harold Wilson
1976–79	James Callaghan
1979–90	**Margaret Thatcher**

'Today we were unlucky,' said the chilling statement from the IRA, 'but remember we only have to be lucky once.' The 1994 bombing of the Grand hotel in Brighton may not have killed the prime minister, but five others died and others were left with lifelong injuries.

1990–97	John Major
1997–2007	Tony Blair
2007–10	Gordon Brown
2010–16	David Cameron
2016–19	**Theresa May**

Asked about the naughtiest thing she'd ever done, May said that she'd once run through a field of wheat with her friends, and that the farmers 'weren't too happy'.

2019–	Boris Johnson

Household Goods in 1962

The basket of 1962 is beginning to look like the basket of today. Alongside new convenient foods there's a fresh emphasis on looking smart inside and outside the home.

Sliced white bread
Chocolate coated biscuits
Dry cleaning
Potato crisps
Crisps entered the basket of goods in 1962, the same year Golden Wonder (bought by Imperial Tobacco) launched cheese and onion flavoured crisps. Golden Wonder, Smith's and soon Walkers fought for the market, and consumption rocketed.

Oven ready chicken
Cuts of halibut
Second-hand car
Welfare milk scheme
Ground coffee
Frozen croquettes
As more homes had freezers and the desire for ready meals increased, frozen food was all the rage. Frozen croquettes were released in the early 1960s and were a resounding success.

Canned fruit salad
Canned fruit salad was designed to use the fruit scraps that couldn't be used in canning. Fruit salad arrived in the 1940s and became one of the most popular canned fruits available. You could even use it to make a fruit salad cake.

TV set rental
Gloss paint
Ceiling paper
Jeans
Latex backed carpet
Refrigerator
Ready-made suit
Terylene slacks
Created in Manchester in 1941, Terylene revolutionised clothing in the 1950s. It was used by Mary Quant to make the original miniskirts, and Ray Davies of The Kinks advertised it.

Around the World When You Turned 35

It's a big news day every day, somewhere in the world. Here are the stories that the media thought you'd want to read in the year of your 35th birthday.

- World's first surviving sextuplets born in South Africa
- US heiress Patty Hearst kidnapped by Symbionese Liberation Army
- Turkish plane crash in forest near Paris kills all 346 on board
- Paris Charles De Gaulle airport opens
- German chancellor Willy Brandt resigns over Stasi spy aide
- Cyclone Tracy kills 71 and devastates Darwin, Australia
- Nixon resigns; Gerald Ford becomes 38th US president
- 8,000 life-size terracotta soldiers unearthed in Xian, China
- Ali KOs Foreman in Zaire Rumble in the Jungle boxing bout
- 3.2-million-year-old pre-human skeleton found in Ethiopia
- Turkish invasion of northern Cyprus leads to island division
- John Lennon plays final live gig at Elton John New York concert
- Philippe Petit walks tightrope between New York's Twin Towers
- Swedish group ABBA's Waterloo wins Eurovision Song Contest
- Marxist coup ousts Haile Selassie, triggering Ethiopian Civil War
- West Germany hosts and wins FIFA World Cup
- USSR expels dissident writer Alexander Solzhenitsyn
- Bloodless Carnation Revolution ends Portugal's fascist regime

Born this year:
- Spanish actress Pénelope Cruz born in Alcobendas near Madrid
- US rapper Lil' Kim born Kimberly Denise Jones in New York
- US actor Leonardo DiCaprio born in Los Angeles
- Australian cricketer Ricky Ponting born in Launceston, Tasmania

Beer of the Seventies

You could haul a seven-pint tin of Watneys Party Seven to a celebration. Someone would be drinking bland Watneys Red, or Courage Tavern ('It's what your right arm's for'). But how about a drop of that cold, refreshing lager you tried on holiday? 'Mine's a pint!' said millions of Brits.

Watneys Party Seven
Whitbread Tankard
Watneys Red
Double Diamond

Carlsberg
The inventor of Carlsberg, JC Jacobsen, gave a Ted Talk on his life philosophy in 2017 – 130 years after he died. He was brought back to life via hologram and even fielded questions from the audience.

Heineken
The Heineken International company owns more than 250 other brands, many of which you'll probably recognise such as Amstel, Desperados and Strongbow.

Tennant's Gold Label

Guinness
When Arthur Guinness started his now-famous business he rented an unused brewery on a 9,000-year lease – though the contract was eventually voided when the company bought the land and surrounding areas to expand the business.

Worthington E
Carling Black Label
Harp
Stella Artois
Ind Coope Super
Younger's Scotch Ale
Bass Charrington

Strongbow
HP Bulmer named his drink after one of the greatest knights in English history, Richard de Clare, who was given the nickname Strongbow.

Long Life

Seventies TV Gameshows

With light entertainment increasingly becoming the bedrock of TV channel success, the seventies saw an explosion of formats from gimmicks to US imports. Which ones got you shouting at the telly?

It's a Knockout
Although this show began in 1966 and it limped on into the new century, the seventies was It's a Knockout's golden age, thanks in no small part to presenter Stuart Hall. The winning teams proceeded to represent the UK at the European final, Jeux Sans Frontières.

I'm Sorry I Haven't a Clue

Jokers Wild

My Music

A Question of Sport
A Question of Sport is the world's longest running TV sports quiz. The first episode was recorded in 1970 in a converted chapel in Rusholme, Manchester, and the show is still recorded in the city as it surpasses 1,300 episodes.

Quote... Unquote

Whodunnit?

Mastermind

Screen Test

Celebrity Squares
Inspired by the game noughts and crosses, Celebrity Squares was based on the US gameshow Hollywood Squares. The original run was presented by Bob Monkhouse, who also returned to host the revival of the show in the 1990s.

Gambit

The Generation Game

The Golden Shot

The Indoor League

Password

Runaround

Sale of the Century

The Sky's the Limit

Winner Takes All

Popular Boys' Names

Just as middle age crept up unnoticed, so the most popular names also evolved. The traditional choices - possibly including yours - were fast losing their appeal to new parents.

Paul
After John, then David, came Paul: the nation's favourite name, but he'd keep the spot for less than a decade.

Mark
David
Andrew
Richard
Christopher
James
Simon
Michael
Matthew
Stephen
Lee
John
Robert
Darren
Daniel
Steven
Jason
Nicholas
Jonathan
Ian
Neil
Peter
Stuart
Anthony
Martin
Kevin

Rising and falling stars:
It's rare that names become popular enough to make the Top 100 only to fall out of favour as quickly as they came. Rarer still to have three flashes-in-the-pan: Glen, Brett and Damian.

Popular Girls' Names

It's a similar story for girls' names. Increasing numbers took their infant inspiration from popular culture. The worlds of music, film and now the internet are all fertile hunting grounds for those in need of inspiration.

Sarah
Claire
Nicola
Emma
Lisa
Joanne
Michelle
Helen
Samantha
At number 9, Samantha's first appearance is among the highest of the century. She'll stay around until 2003.

Karen
Amanda
Rachel
Louise
Julie
Clare
Rebecca
Sharon
Victoria
Caroline
Susan
Alison
Catherine
Elizabeth
Deborah
Donna
Tracey
Tracy

Rising and falling stars:
Just like the boys, several names are all-too-briefly on the lips of many new parents: Vanessa, Nichola, Tara, Clair and Sonia.

F1 Champions

If you fancy your chances in Formula One, start young. Sebastian Vettel won at 23. *El Maestro*, Juan Manuel Fangio, is the oldest winner to date, at 46. The field is wide open for an older champ, right?

Graham Hill 🏆 (1962,68)
Jim Clark 🏆 (1963,65)
John Surtees 🏆 (1964)
In 1965, Surtees crashed during practice. He was crushed by the car and suffered severe injuries that left one side of his body four inches shorter than the other.

Jack Brabham 🏆 (1959-60,66)
Denny Hulme 🏆 (1967)
Jackie Stewart 🏆 (1969,71,73)
Jochen Rindt 🏆 (1970)
Rindt was awarded the Drivers' Championship posthumously after crashing at Monza, having built an unassailable season lead. A poorly-fitted crash barrier was the main cause of death. He was the third F1 driver to die that year.

Emerson Fittipaldi 🏆 (1972,74)
Niki Lauda 🏆 (1975,77,84)
Niki Lauda was also an aviation entrepreneur, founding three airlines in Austria. He also held a commercial pilot's licence.

James Hunt 🏆 (1976)
Mario Andretti 🏆 (1978)
Jody Scheckter 🏆 (1979)
Alan Jones 🏆 (1980)
Nelson Piquet 🏆 (1981,83,87)
Nelson Piquet lost his civilian driving licence in 2007 due to numerous speeding and parking offences. He was ordered to attend a week of lessons and pass an exam.

Keke Rosberg 🏆 (1982)
Alain Prost 🏆 (1985-6,89,93)

Fashion in the Seventies

The decade that taste forgot? Or a kickback against the sixties and an explosion of individuality? Skirts got shorter (and longer). Block colours and peasant chic vied with sequins and disco glamour. How many of your seventies outfits would you still wear today?

Flares
Platform shoes
Laura Ashley
While working as a secretary, Laura Ashley was inspired to produce printed fabric after seeing a display at the Victoria and Albert Museum. Struggling to make a profit, Laura Ashley and her husband and children once lived in tents in Wales for six months.

Gucci
Diane Von Furstenberg
Tie Dye
Kaftans
Brought to western culture via the hippie trail, the kaftan's popularity was boosted further when Elizabeth Taylor wore a kaftan-inspired dress for her second wedding to Richard Burton in 1975.

Liza Minnelli
Lurex and suede
David Bowie
Afro, braids or a perm
Jumpsuit
Sequin hot pants
Moon boots
Double denim
Double denim garnered the nickname the 'Canadian tuxedo' after Bing Crosby was refused entry to a hotel in Vancouver because he wore a denim ensemble. Levi subsequently designed Crosby a denim tuxedo.

Vivienne Westwood
Previously a primary school teacher, Vivienne Westwood lived in an ex-council flat in Clapham until 2000. Her son from her relationship with Malcolm McLaren founded lingerie brand Agent Provocateur.

Household Goods in 1970

Frozen foods and eating out swallow up an increasingly larger share of the family budget in the seventies. Or how about a day trip (don't forget your AA membership and your mac), then home for a sweet sherry?

Frozen chicken
Mushrooms
Frozen beans
Sherry
Sherry consumption peaked in the UK in the 1970s following the development of sweet versions - often using added syrups or sugars - known as creams and developed for British palates.

Night storage heater
Plastic Mackintosh
MOT test
Introduced in 1960, the MOT was designed to test the brakes, lights, and steering of all vehicles over 10 years old. This was progressively reduced to every three years by 1967, and the test changed to include tyres.

State school meal
Canteen meal
Cup of tea
The 1970s saw a significant increase in eating out, so a cup of tea was added to the basket. Despite Britain's reputation as tea lovers, coffee sales overtook tea sales for the first time in 1986.

Cafe sandwich
Local authority rent
Local authority rent was added to the basket of goods in the 1970s; by 1979, 42% of Britons lived in council homes.

Paper handkerchiefs
Auto association subs
Keg of ale
Fresh cream
Gammon
While gammon gained popularity during the 1970s due to its unlikely pairing with pineapple rings, the word 'gammon' is now also used as an insult towards the political right, coined in response to 'snowflake'.

Post-war Chocolate

You'll find nearly all of these on the supermarket shelves, even though the most recently invented chocolate bar here was brought to market thirty years ago. Gulp.

1948	Fudge
1951	**Bounty** If you wanted to sell a chocolate bar with curved ends and swirls on the top, in theory there's nothing that maker Mars could do to stop you: the shape was decreed not distinctive enough to trademark in 2009. Do check with a lawyer first, though.
1957	Munchies
1958	Picnic
1962	**After Eight Mint Chocolate Thins** A billion of these are churned out every year (although we've never heard anyone call them chocolate thins).
1962	Topic
1963	Toffee Crisp
1967	Twix
1970	Chomp
1970	Curly Wurly
1973	Freddo
1976	**Double Decker** Double Deckers contain raisins, don't they? Not any more: they were removed from the recipe during the eighties.
1976	Starbar
1976	**Yorkie** 'It's not for girls,' said the adverts. The sexist marketing of Yorkie reached its peak – or trough – in 2005 with special pink editions. By 2011 the complaints outweighed the commercial advantage. The 'men only' angle was dropped.
1978	Lion Bar
1980	Drifter
1983	**Wispa** For twenty years, Wispa was the go-to Aero alternative. But then in 2003 it was gone. A predictable outcry followed and in 2007 it was back on the shelves. Phew.
1992	Time Out

Books of the Decade

Family, friends, TV, and more: there are as many midlife distractions as there are books on the shelf. Did you get drawn in by these bestsellers, all published in your thirties?

1969	Slaughterhouse-Five by Kurt Vonnegut
1969	Portnoy's Complaint by Philip Roth
1969	The Godfather by Mario Puzo
1969	The French Lieutenant's Woman by John Fowles
1969	Them by Joyce Carol Oates
1970	Deliverance by James Dickey
1971	An Accidental Man by Iris Murdoch
1971	The Day of the Jackal by Frederick Forsyth
1972	**Watership Down by Richard Adams** Watership Down was the first story Adams ever wrote, at the age of 52, based on tales he told his daughters in the car.
1973	Gravity's Rainbow by Thomas Pynchon
1973	Crash: A Novel by J G Ballard
1974	**Tinker, Tailor, Soldier, Spy by John le Carré** David Cornwell, the man behind the pseudonym John le Carré, drew on his personal experience working for MI5 and MI6. He appeared as an extra in the film of the book.
1974	**Carrie by Stephen King** Carrie was King's first novel, published when he was 26. He disliked the first draft and threw it in the bin; his wife found it and encouraged him to continue with the story.
1974	The Bottle Factory Outing by Beryl Bainbridge
1975	Shogun by James Clavell
1975	The Periodic Table by Primo Levi
1976	**Interview with the Vampire by Anne Rice** Rice wrote the novel following the death of her five-year-old daughter from leukaemia; the character of vampire child Claudia is inspired by her.
1977	Song of Solomon by Toni Morrison
1977	The Shining by Stephen King
1978	The World According to Garp by John Irving
1978	The Sea, The Sea by Iris Murdoch

Around the World When You Turned 40

Which of these international news events were on your radar as you clocked up four decades on the planet?

- ✦ Pol Pot's brutal regime ends as Vietnam takes Cambodian capital
- ✦ Iranian radicals storm US Embassy in Tehran, taking 90 hostages
- ✦ Dutch firm Philips unveils first compact disc and player
- ✦ Shah of Iran flees country as Muslim fundamentalists take power
- ✦ First black-led government of Zimbabwe-Rhodesia takes power
- ✦ China institutes one child per family rule
- ✦ Ixtoc well blowout off Mexican coast causes massive oil spill
- ✦ Last British soldier leaves Malta after 166 years of UK rule
- ✦ US space station Skylab falls to Earth in Australia and Pacific
- ✦ Ugandan dictator Idi Amin overthrown
- ✦ Nuclear melt-down at Three Mile Island plant in Pennsylvania, USA
- ✦ US and USSR sign SALT II nuclear arms reduction treaty
- ✦ Two families escape East Berlin in homemade hot-air balloon
- ✦ Snow falls in world's hottest desert the Sahara
- ✦ War breaks out as Chinese troops invade northern Vietnam
- ✦ Freak storm lashes 300 yachts in UK's Fastnet race – 19 drown
- ✦ Pink Floyd's concept album The Wall released
- ✦ Personal stereo tape-deck Sony Walkman goes on sale in Japan

Born this year:
- ☙ Ireland rugby captain Brian O'Driscoll born in Dublin
- ☙ Oscar-winning actor Heath Ledger born Perth, Australia
- ☙ Homeland actress Claire Danes born in New York, USA
- ☙ US comedian/actor Kevin Hart born in Philadelphia, Pennsylvania

Around the UK

(40)

Here are the headline stories from across the country in the year you hit 40.

- ✦ Sex Pistols Sid Vicious dies of drug overdose
- ✦ Lord Mountbatten killed by IRA bomb
- ✦ Margaret Thatcher becomes UK's first female prime minister
- ✦ IRA blast at Warrenpoint near Newry kills 18 British soldiers
- ✦ UK's first public naturist beach opens in Brighton
- ✦ The Times publishes again after year-long dispute
- ✦ Elton John first western rock star to perform in USSR
- ✦ UK controls on buying and using foreign currency lifted
- ✦ Lorry drivers' strike causes food and fuel shortages
- ✦ Shadow Northern Ireland Secretary Airey Neave killed by car bomb (right)
- ✦ Anti-racism protester Blair Peach killed by police
- ✦ St Lucia gains independence from UK
- ✦ Athlete Sebastian Coe sets new record for mile
- ✦ First man-powered plane crosses English Channel
- ✦ Anthony Blunt 'fourth man' in Cambridge spy ring
- ✦ Amusement park Thorpe Park opens in Surrey
- ✦ Isle of Man marks 1,000 years of Tynwald parliament
- ✦ Former Liberal leader Jeremy Thorpe cleared of attempted murder
- ✦ Government-TUC agreement ends Winter of Discontent
- ✦ London Underground's Jubilee line opens
- ✦ Scots vote for devolution; Wales says no

Born this year:
- ✺ Actress Rosamund Pike born in west London
- ✺ Rugby union star Jonny Wilkinson born in Frimley, Surrey
- ✺ Jazz musician Jamie Cullum born in Rochford, Essex

Keystone Pictures USA/ZUMAPRESS.com/Mary Evans

Airey Neave, a WWII war hero who became Shadow Secretary of State for Northern Ireland, was murdered by the Irish National Liberation Army on 30 March 1979. A magnetic car bomb killed Neave as he left the Palace of Westminster. Margaret Thatcher, who's campaign to become leader was managed by Neave, called him 'staunch, brave, true, strong.' She is accompanied above at Neave's funeral service by Ian Gow, Thatcher's private secretary and colleague of Neave. Gow was assassinated in 1990.

The Biggest Hits When You Were 40

Big tunes for a big birthday: how many of them enticed your middle-aged party guests onto the dance floor?

YMCA 🎵 **Village People**
The Village People were livid at Donald Trump's use of their hit song at his rallies, labelling it as abusive.

Heart of Glass 🎵 Blondie

Tragedy 🎵 Bee Gees

I Will Survive 🎵 **Gloria Gaynor**
I Will Survive was added to the national recording registry in the Library of Congress in Washington. Each year, 25 decade-old pieces of music are added to the collection based on their cultural and social impact.

Bright Eyes 🎵 **Art Garfunkel**
Bright Eyes was featured on the feature-length movie adaptation of Watership Down.

Ring My Bell 🎵 Anita Ward

I Don't Like Mondays 🎵 The Boomtown Rats

We Don't Talk Anymore 🎵 Cliff Richard

Cars 🎵 **Gary Numan**
It only took 30 minutes for Gary Numan to come up with this song, his biggest hit.

Message in a Bottle 🎵 The Police

One Day at a Time 🎵 Lena Martell

Walking on the Moon 🎵 The Police

Another Brick in the Wall 🎵 Pink Floyd

Popular Food in the 1970s

Roll out the hostess trolley, seventies food is ready to be served. If it's not highly processed, artificially coloured, moulded and served in a novelty dish, is it even food? Still, most of it went down very well with the kids – and still does today, given half a chance.

Lemon meringue pie

Cheese and pineapple

Black Forest Gâteau

The Black Forest Gâteau is named after the kirsch alcohol made from Black Forest sour cherries, rather than the Black Forest region in Germany.

Dream Topping

Mateus Rose, Liebfraumilch and Chianti

Cornetto

Cornetto cones were created by Spica, an Italian ice-cream company, in 1976. The company was bought by Unilever not long after, who then marketed the dessert in Europe.

Quavers

Quiche

Unlike the gâteau above, quiche Lorraine *was* named after the area in which it was created. It is considered a French dish, even though Lorraine was under German rule at the time.

Pot Noodle

The original Pot Noodle made in 1979 did not contain a sauce sachet – these were only added in 1992.

Fondue

Smash

Scampi in a basket

Banoffee pie

Chili con carne

Chili is the state dish of Texas, where many people think the recipe originated. Before WWII, hundreds of individual parlours all insisted they had their own secret recipe.

Prawn cocktails

Profiteroles

The Full English Breakfast

Cars of the 1970s

How did you get around in the seventies? Was it in one of the decade's fancy new Range Rovers, or perhaps something more modest like a Morris Marina? Here are the decade's most famous (and infamous) cars.

Ford Capri

Vauxhall HC Viva

Ford Escort

Introduced in 1968, the Ford Escort went on to be the best-selling car in Britain in the 1980s and 1990s. The car was brought back into the spotlight in 2013, when it was featured in Fast & Furious 6.

Jaguar XJ

Triumph TR7

Austin Allegro

Austin Maxi

The Austin Maxi was the first British five-door hatchback, and one of the first cars to be featured on the BBC's Wheelbase show.

Ford Cortina

Ford Granada

Designed as a European executive car, the Granada was popular for taxi and police car use. It was also modified for use as a hearse and limousine, and was often seen in The Sweeney.

Leyland Princess

Triumph Dolomite

Vauxhall Cavalier

Range Rover

Morris Marina

The popular Morris Marina is ranked amongst the worst cars ever built. The car was released with poor suspension, chronic understeer, and windscreen wipers fitted the wrong way round.

Hillman Avenger

Saab 99

Datsun Sunny

BMW 316

Volkswagen Beetle

Affectionately known as the bug in English-speaking countries, it is called turtle in Bolivia, frog in Indonesia, and hunchback in Poland.

Household Goods in 1980

Mortgage interest rates were around 15% as we went into the eighties, not much lower as we left, and added to our basket in 1980. If you had any money left over perhaps you were spending it on home perms, cement and lamb's liver!

Lamb's liver

Tea bags
Tea is one of the few items included in the basket since the start. Tea bags were added in 1980; loose tea was removed in 2002.

Smash
Smash sales soared following the 1974 TV adverts featuring the Smash Martians. It was replaced in 1987 by oven chips.

Cider

Wine

Mortgage Interest

White spirit

Cement

Toilet seat

Electric plug

Colour TV
Colour TV sets outnumbered black and white sets in 1976.

Record player

Cassette recorder
Cassette recorders were first introduced by Philips in the 1960s and were originally intended for dictation and journalists.

Electric hairdryer

Carpet sweeper

Continental quilt

Drycell batteries

Colour photo film

Briefcase

Home perm

National Trust fees
Membership to the National Trust significantly increased throughout the 1980s (around 5.6 million people are members today). The Giant's Causeway is the most visited national attraction.

Olympic Medallists in Your Life

With seven gold medals, Jason Kenny is without equal while the unique achievements of Laura Trott – now Mrs Kenny – brings the household tally to twelve. Meanwhile, over at the Paralympics, swimmer-cyclist Sarah Storey has an incredible 17 gold medals. And medals of all colours? Here are the heroes of Team GB at the Summer Olympics.

Jason Kenny (9) Cycling
Bradley Wiggins (8) Cycling
Britain's most decorated Olympian until Kenny took the crown in Tokyo, Wiggo acquired various nicknames throughout his career. In France he was referred to as 'Le Gentleman', while the Dutch apparently called him 'The Banana with the Sideburns'.

Chris Hoy (7) Cycling
Laura Kenny (6) Cycling
Our most successful female Olympian with five gold medals, Trott (now Kenny) began life with a collapsed lung and asthma.

Steve Redgrave (6) Rowing
Max Whitlock (6) Gymnastics
Charlotte Dujardin (6) Equestrianism
Ben Ainslie (5) Sailing
Known for his hot temper, Ben Ainslie has accused competitors of teaming up against him. He was disqualified from the world championships in Australia for confronting a photographer who Ainslie felt had impeded his progress.

Adam Peaty (5) Swimming
Katherine Grainger (5) Rowing
Grainger is the first British woman to win medals at five successive Olympic games, from Sydney to Rio.

Mo Farah (4) Athletics
Matthew Pinsent (4) Rowing
Ed Clancy (4) Cycling
Ian Stark (4) Equestrianism
Louis Smith (4) Gymnastics
Becky Adlington (4) Swimming
Seb Coe (4) Athletics
Ginny Leng (4) Equestrianism

Keystone Pictures USA/ZUMAPRESS.com/Mary Evans

It's striking that our most decorated Olympians did so in recent decades. Of the 18 athletes earning four medals or more since you were born, Seb Coe came off the starting blocks first: he won his first medal at the 1980 Moscow Olympics at the age of 23 (shortly after breaking the 1,000 metre record in Oslo, above).

Run the slide rule over every modern Olympics, starting in 1896, and only six more GB athletes have achieved the same phenomenal success.

Winter Olympics Venues Since You Were Born

Unless you're an athlete or winter sports fan, the Winter Olympics can slip past almost unnoticed. These are the venues; can you remember the host countries and years?

Lillehammer
Cortina d'Ampezzo
Oslo
Salt Lake City
Sapporo
Albertville
The last Games to be held in the same year as the Summer Olympics, with the next Winter Olympics held two years later.

Turin
Grenoble
Sarajevo
Lake Placid
Sochi
Innsbruck (twice)
This usually snowy city experienced its mildest winter in 60 years; the army was called in to transport snow and ice from the mountains. Nevertheless, twelve years later, the Winter Olympics were back.

Squaw Valley
Nagano
St Moritz
The first Winter Olympics to be held for 12 years and named the 'Games of Renewal'; Japan and Germany were not invited.

Calgary
Vancouver
PyeongChang

Answers: Lillehammer: Norway, 1994; Cortina d'Ampezzo: Italy, 1956; Oslo: Norway, 1952; Salt Lake City: USA, 2002; Sapporo: Japan, 1972; Albertville: France, 1992; Turin: Italy, 2006; Grenoble: France, 1968; Sarajevo: Yugoslavia, 1984; Lake Placid: USA, 1980; Sochi: Russia, 2014; Innsbruck: Austria, 1964; Squaw Valley: USA, 1960; Nagano: Japan, 1998; St Moritz: Switzerland, 1948; Calgary: Canada, 1988; Innsbruck: Austria, 1976; Vancouver: Canada, 2010; PyeongChang: South Korea, 2018

Fashion in the Eighties

Eighties fashion was many things, but subtle wasn't one of them. Brash influences were everywhere from aerobics to Wall Street, from pop princesses to preppy polo shirts. The result was chaotic, but fun. How many eighties throwbacks still lurk in your closet?

Shoulder pads or puffed sleeves

Scrunchies
Patented in 1987 by nightclub singer Rommy Revson, the first scrunchie was designed using the waistband of her pyjama bottoms. The softer alternative to hair bands was named after Revson's dog Scunchie (no, that's not a typo).

Conical bras
Inspired by 1950s bullet bras, Jean Paul Gaultier introduced the cone bra in 1984. As a child he fashioned the bra for his teddy bear; years later he reworked the look for Madonna's Blonde Ambition tour in 1990.

Acid wash jeans

Slogan t-shirts
Designer Katharine Hamnett introduced slogan t-shirts, famously revealing one displaying an anti-nuclear statement when meeting Margaret Thatcher in 1984. Wham opted for 'Choose Life'; for Frankie Goes to Hollywood it was 'Frankie Says Relax'.

Leotards and leg-warmers
Leg-warmers reached the masses following the release of Fame and Flashdance, as well as Jane Fonda exercise videos. Nowadays, leg-warmers are even worn by babies while they have their nappies changed.

Deely boppers, bangle earrings or a polka dot hair bow

Pedal pushers or leggings

Guyliner

Levi 501s

Pixie boots

Ra-ra skirt and PVC belts

Dr Martens
Dr Martens were designed by a German soldier to aid the recovery of his broken foot. Pete Townshend of The Who was the first rock star to wear the boots on stage, and the shoe was adopted by numerous subcultures.

World Buildings

Buildings that are known the world over for all the right (and the wrong) reasons and were opened before you turned 40.

1941	Australian War Memorial, Canberra
1943	The Pentagon, Arlington, Virginia
1943	**Jefferson Memorial, Washington DC** Designed at the request of Franklin D Roosevelt and modelled after the Pantheon of Rome. The 19-foot bronze statue of Jefferson was painted plaster at the time of the Memorial's dedication due to wartime shortages.
1947	Hearst Castle, San Simeon, California
1955	**Hiroshima Peace Museum, Hiroshima** Built following the atomic bombing of Hiroshima as an enduring symbol of peace and to educate, the museum receives over a million visitors each year.
1958	Tokyo Tower, Tokyo
1958	Expo '58 World's Fair, Brussels
1958	Seagram Building, New York
1959	**The Guggenheim, New York** Architect Frank Lloyd Wright produced over 700 sketches of the museum. Upon opening, Woody Allen commented that it looked like a giant lavatory basin.
1961	**Space Needle, Seattle** Built for the 1962 World's Fair. Early shape designs included a tethered balloon and a cocktail shaker before the iconic final design was chosen.
1968	Madison Square Garden, New York City, New York
1969	John Hancock Center, Chicago
1973	Sears Tower, Chicago, Illinois
1973	World Trade Center, New York
1973	**Sydney Opera House, Sydney** The estimated cost for the construction was AU$7m (£4m). It ended up costing AU$102m (£59m), and took 14 years to build rather than the four years planned.
1976	CN Tower, Toronto
1977	Pompidou Centre, Paris

Around the UK

How many of these big national stories do you remember unfolding live on TV and radio?

- ✦ Guildford Four cleared of IRA bombings after 15 years in jail
- ✦ Band Aid II's new version of charity single tops Christmas charts
- ✦ Electronic tagging first trialled in the UK
- ✦ UK's first satellite television service Sky TV goes on air
- ✦ IRA bomb kills and injures 32 at Marines music school in Deal
- ✦ Army steps into breach during ambulance workers' pay strike
- ✦ Two trains collide at Purley, Surrey, leaving six dead
- ✦ 47 dead after M1 plane crash near Kegworth, Leicestershire
- ✦ 20 million watch as Dirty Den leaves EastEnders
- ✦ 51 die when party boat Marchioness collides on Thames
- ✦ British author Salman Rushdie put under Ayatollah death threat
- ✦ Inmates stage rooftop protest at Cheshire's Risley remand centre
- ✦ Crush at Sheffield's Hillsborough stadium kills 96 football fans
- ✦ Tube staff strike over plans for driver-only operated trains
- ✦ House of Commons proceedings televised for first time
- ✦ Government ends dockers' 'jobs for life' legislation
- ✦ Channel Tunnel workers strike for better pay and conditions
- ✦ Princess Diana opens Landmark AIDS Centre in London
- ✦ Yorkshire Ripper's wife wins libel action against Private Eye
- ✦ BBC's Dr Who series cancelled after 26 seasons

Born this year:
- ⚭ Olympic gold swimmer Rebecca Adlington born in Mansfield
- ⚭ England and Southampton footballer Theo Walcott born in London
- ⚭ Heavyweight boxing champion Anthony Joshua born in Watford
- ⚭ Harry Potter actor Daniel Radcliffe born in London, England

Around the World When You Turned 50

We're no longer lost in the mists of time: here is a list of international news stories from your more recent past. Do you remember where you were when you first heard about them?

✦ George HW Bush sworn in as 41st US president
✦ South Africa's President Botha meets prisoner Nelson Mandela
✦ Nintendo releases handheld video game console Game Boy
✦ Icelanders celebrate legalisation of beer after 74 years
✦ 'Tank Man' stands up to army in Beijing's Tiananmen Square
✦ East Germans flock to border as Berlin Wall comes down
✦ NASA launches Galileo spacecraft to study Jupiter
✦ FW de Klerk succeeds Botha as South African president
✦ Overthrown Romanian dictator Ceauşescu executed by firing squad
✦ UK inventor Tim Berners-Lee creates World Wide Web
✦ Oil tanker Exxon Valdez spills millions of gallons off Alaska
✦ Bush and Gorbachev declare end of Cold War at Malta summit
✦ 14th Dalai Lama Tenzin Gyatso wins Nobel Peace Prize
✦ France celebrates 200th anniversary of storming of Bastille
✦ Revolutions in Eastern Bloc countries end communist regimes
✦ Iran's ayatollah urges Muslims to kill UK author Salman Rushdie
✦ Hoffman-Cruise film Rain Man wins four Oscars
✦ Infamous US serial killer Ted Bundy executed in electric chair

Born this year:
⚭ US politician Alexandria Ocasio-Cortez born in New York
⚭ US pop singer Taylor Swift born in West Reading, Pennsylvania
⚭ Grammy-winning DJ Avicii born Tim Bergling in Stockholm, Sweden

Grand Designs

Governments around the world spent much of the 20th century nation building (and rebuilding). Here is a selection of striking civil engineering achievements between the ages of 0 and 30.

1939	**Saltdean Lido, Brighton** This critically acclaimed lido also proved popular with the public, but it was only open for three summer seasons; it was forced to close after German pilots opened fire on the pool's visitors. Work is underway to restore it.
1940	Ataturk Bridge, Istanbul
1943	Bletchley Park D Block, Milton Keynes
1945	**Waterloo Bridge, London** Following numerous problems, the original bridge was demolished in the 1930s. Constructed during World War II, the bridge was nicknamed the 'Ladies' Bridge', as the workforce who built the bridge was largely female.
1946	Pontins, Weston-super-Mare
1946	Lakihegy Radio Tower, Hungary (rebuilt)
1955	Disneyland Castle, Anaheim, California
1955	Battersea Power Station, London
1959	**M1 Motorway, London & Leeds** The M1 was the second motorway built in the UK, and it was the first motorway to join two cities. The first section opened in 1959, and the most recent section was added in 1999.
1959	Kariba Dam, Kariba
1962	Butlins, Minehead
1965	Mont Blanc Tunnel, France & Italy
1965	Zeeland Bridge, Netherlands
1966	**Almondsbury Interchange, Bristol & Gloucester** The Almondsbury Interchange was the first example of a four-level stack in the UK, and remains one of only three of its kind in the country.
1967	Second Blackwall Tunnel, London
1969	Humber Refinery, Northern Lincolnshire

Household Goods in 1987

The shelves, fridges and freezers are piled high with convenience foods. What did we do with all that extra time we'd saved? First, dig out the indigestion tablets. Then tackle a spot of DIY and finally move house, it seems!

Squash racket
The classic eighties sport. Prince Philip played squash to relax while Queen Elizabeth II was in labour with Prince Charles.

Muesli

Spaghetti

Jam doughnuts

Swiss roll

Beefburgers

Mince

Garlic sausage

Frozen prawns

Brie

Red Leicester
Originally called Leicestershire Cheese, the cheese was renamed Red Leicester after World War II to differentiate it from 'White Leicester' made during rationing when the use of colouring agents was banned.

Conifer

Frozen curry and rice

Fish and chips
Synonymous with British cuisine and described by Winston Churchill as 'the good companions', fish and chips were exempt from rationing during World War II, as the government feared any limitations would damage the morale of the nation.

VHS recorder

Ready mixed filler

Home telephone
The popularity of mobile phones has led to a decrease of landlines. Only 73% of British households had a landline used to make calls in 2020.

Fabric conditioner

Estate agent fees

Indigestion tablets

Books of the Decade

By our forties, most of us have decided what we like to read. But occasionally a book can break the spell, revealing the delights of other genres. Did any of these newly published books do that for you?

1979	**The Hitchhiker's Guide to the Galaxy by Douglas Adams** If 42 is the meaning of life, what's the meaning of 42? Nothing. Adams said it was simply a random number he chose. There's a message in there somewhere…
1979	A Bend in the River by V S Naipaul
1979	Sophie's Choice by William Styron
1980	A Confederacy of Dunces by John Kennedy Toole
1980	The Name of the Rose by Umberto Eco
1981	Midnight's Children by Salman Rushdie
1982	The Color Purple by Alice Walker
1982	**Schindler's Ark by Thomas Keneally** Keneally wrote Schindler's Ark – later retitled Schindler's List – after he met Holocaust survivor Leopold Page. Schindler is credited with saving over 1,000 lives.
1983	The Colour of Magic by Terry Pratchett
1983	Waterland by Graham Swift
1984	Money by Martin Amis
1984	Neuromancer by William Gibson
1984	The Wasp Factory by Iain Banks
1985	**The Handmaid's Tale by Margaret Atwood** The Communist reign of Nicolae Ceaușescu in Romania partially inspired Atwood to write The Handmaid's Tale. While he was in power, women had to have four babies; abortions were illegal, contraception was banned, and women were examined for signs of pregnancy at work.
1985	Blood Meridian by Cormac McCarthy
1985	Perfume by Patrick Suskind
1986	The Old Devils by Kingsley Amis
1986	It by Stephen King
1987	Beloved by Toni Morrison
1987	Bonfire of the Vanities by Tom Wolfe
1988	Satanic Verses by Salman Rushdie

US Vice Presidents in Your Lifetime

The linchpin of a successful presidency, a springboard to become POTUS, or both? Here are the men – and the woman – who have shadowed the most powerful person in the world in your lifetime. (President in brackets.)

1933-41	**John Garner** (Franklin D Roosevelt) His nickname was Cactus Jack and he lived to be 98 years old, making him the longest-lived VP to date.
1941-45	Henry A Wallace (Franklin D Roosevelt)
1945	Harry S Truman (Franklin D Roosevelt)
1949-53	**Alben W Barkley** (Harry S Truman) Barkley died of a heart attack during a convention speech three years after the end of his term.
1953-61	Richard Nixon (Dwight Eisenhower)
1961-63	Lyndon B Johnson (John F Kennedy)
1965-69	**Hubert Humphrey** (Lyndon Johnson) Christmas 1977: with just weeks to live, the former VP made goodbye calls. One was to Richard Nixon, the man who had beaten Humphrey to become president in 1968. Sensing Nixon's unhappiness at his status as Washington outcast, Humphrey invited him to take a place of honour at the funeral he knew was fast approaching.
1969-73	**Spiro Agnew (right)**
1973-74	Gerald Ford
1974-77	Nelson Rockefeller
1977-81	Walter Mondale
1981-89	**George HW Bush** He is only the second vice president to win the presidency while holding the office of vice president.
1989-93	**Dan Quayle** You say potato, Quayle said potatoe: he famously told a student to add an 'e' during a 1992 school visit.
1993-2001	Al Gore
2001-09	Dick Cheney
2009-17	Joe Biden
2017-20	Mike Pence
2020-	Kamala Harris

Mary Evans / Everett Collection

Spiro Agnew resigned in 1973, the second VP to quit in America's history (the first was John Calhoun in 1932). He stepped down after being charged with tax evasion and taking bribes. He covered his legal debts with a loan from friend Frank Sinatra. In 1983, Agnew was compelled to repay $268,000: the money he had taken in bribes, plus interest.

Stamps in the Seventies

By the seventies, any hobbyist intent on keeping a complete ongoing collection needed deep pockets (or a rich uncle). New stamps were churned out several times a year and the subjects became ever more esoteric: not just flowers and trees but racket sports, or paintings of horse races. Was your album gathering dust by then?

1970	Commonwealth Games
1971	British rural architecture
1972	Polar explorers
1972	Village churches
1972	Royal Silver Wedding celebration
1973	Plant a Tree Year
1973	County Cricket
1973	**400th anniversary of the birth of Inigo Jones** Not a household name by today's standards, Jones was an early and influential architect. He designed Covent Garden Square and parts of St Paul's Cathedral.
1973	Royal Wedding (Princess Anne and Mark Phillips)
1973	Britain's entry into the EC
1974	Medieval Warriors
1975	Sailing
1975	100 years since the birth of Jane Austen
1976	100 years of the telephone
1976	**British cultural traditions** The four chosen were a Morris dancer, a Scots piper, a Welsh harpist and an Archdruid.
1977	Racket sports
1977	Silver Jubilee
1977	Wildlife
1978	**Energy resources** In an era before renewable energy the choices made were oil, coal, natural gas and electricity.
1978	Horses
1979	Dogs
1979	Spring wild flowers
1979	Paintings of horse races
1979	150 years of the Metropolitan Police

More Things People Do Now...

... that nobody ever did when you were small – because they couldn't, wouldn't, or definitely shouldn't!

✦ **Place a bet *during* a sporting event**
This became popular in the 1990s; first on the phone, now online.

✦ Turn on underfloor heating

✦ **Buy soft toilet rolls**
In 1942, a wonder was created in Walthamstow's St Andrews Road, one for which the bottoms of the world owe a huge debt: two-ply, soft toilet roll ('It's splinter-free'!). It was christened Andrex.

✦ Talk to a smart speaker

✦ Clean up dog poo (not doing it has been an offence since 1996)

✦ Listen to a podcast

✦ **Do a Sudoku puzzle**
How many Japanese words do you know? Tsunami? Karaoke? Sake? In 2005, you likely added another: Sudoku (meaning 'single number'). The puzzle originated in the USA – but was popularised by Wayne Gould, a Hong Kong judge from New Zealand who found a translated version in a Tokyo bookshop.

✦ **Cheat in a pub quiz**
Which two capital cities mean the same in different languages? Who knows? Google knows, and a quick trip to the loo (phone in hand) is a modern phenomenon. (The answer is Sierra Leone's Freetown and Gabon's Libreville – but of course you knew that.)

✦ Order something for same day delivery

✦ Use chopsticks

✦ Fly a drone

✦ **Never watch live TV**
Owning a TV but not watching any live programmes (just streamed content) might sound odd. But that is the reality for many – and around 1.5m have ditched the TV completely.

✦ Eat in the street

✦ Buy water

✦ **Use SatNav**
In the 1980s, Ronald Reagan permitted civilian use of satellites for navigation and opened up a world in which we never need to get lost again – unless we want to. Or the USA pulls the plug.

✦ Argue for hours with strangers you'll never meet

A Lifetime of Progress

It's easy to lose sight of the breadth and pace of life-enhancing inventions made as you grew up – although some of these didn't stand the test of time! These are the biggies before you turned 50.

1962	Red LED
1964	Plasma display
1965	Hypertext (http)
1966	Computer RAM
1967	**Computer mouse** Doug Engelbart patented an early version of his 'X-Y indicator' in 1967. By the time a (very large) mouse became available with a Xerox computer in 1981, the patent had expired.
1967	Hand-held calculator
1969	Laser printer
1971	Email
1973	Mobile phone
1976	Apple Computer
1979	Barcodes
1979	Compact disc
1982	**Emoticons** The inventor of the smiley emoticon hands out 'Smiley' cookies every Sept 19th – the anniversary of its first use.
1983	Internet
1983	Microsoft Word
1985	**Sinclair C5** Despite a body and a chassis designed by Lotus and assembled by Hoover, the ahead-of-its-time Sinclair C5 was plagued with problems including poor battery life, the inability to climb gentle hills and safety concerns.
1986	Mir Space Station
1988	**Internet virus** The first Internet worm was specifically designed to go after passwords. Its inventor was the son of the man who invented computer passwords.
1989	World Wide Web
1990	Hubble space telescope

The Biggest Hits When You Were 50

Fifty: an age when your musical taste is largely settled and modern music can lose its appeal…but how many do you know and how many do you like?

Belfast Child ♂ Simple Minds
Simple Minds took the melody for this song from the Irish traditional number, She Moves Through the Fair.

Too Many Broken Hearts ♂ Jason Donovan
Like a Prayer ♂ Madonna
Like a Prayer received its worldwide debut as part of a Pepsi commercial during the Grammys. Pepsi had to withdraw the ad due to controversy over the video.

Eternal Flame ♂ The Bangles
The Bangles had to change their name from the Bangs after a New Jersey band with the same name came to light. For a while they were simply Bangles, before later adding 'The'.

Hand on Your Heart ♂ Kylie Minogue
Sealed with a Kiss ♂ Jason Donovan
Ride On Time ♂ Black Box
That's What I Like ♂ Jive Bunny
All Around the World ♂ Lisa Stansfield
You Got It ♂ New Kids on the Block
Do They Know It's Christmas? ♂ Band Aid II
Do you know the only band to feature on both Band Aid and Band Aid II? Bananarama.

Back to Life ♂ Soul II Soul

Gameshow Hosts of the Seventies and Eighties

What do points make? I've started so I'll finish. Shut that door! You can't beat a bit of Bully! The catchphrases echo down the ages from these much-loved TV favourites.

David Vine ➤ (A Question of Sport)
Stuart Hall ➤ (It's a Knockout)
Anneka Rice ➤ (Treasure Hunt)
Kenneth Kendall ➤ (Treasure Hunt)
Cilla Black ➤ (Blind Date)
Born Priscilla White, the stage name of Cilla Black came about by mistake. Featured in the first issue of Mersey Beat newspaper, the journalist accidentally called her Cilla Black. Cilla liked the name and opted to keep it.

Barry Cryer ➤ (Jokers Wild)
Nicholas Parsons ➤ (Just a Minute, Sale of the Century)
Jim Bowen ➤ (Bullseye)
After completing his national service in the bomb disposal unit, Jim Bowen worked as a teacher and was promoted to deputy head, but gave up teaching once he appeared on The Comedians alongside Mike Reid.

Mike Read ➤ (Pop Quiz)
David Coleman ➤ (A Question of Sport)
Prof. Heinz Wolff ➤ (The Great Egg Race)
Bob Holness ➤ (Blockbusters)
Magnus Magnusson ➤ (Mastermind)
Angela Rippon ➤ (Masterteam)
Noel Edmonds ➤ (Telly Addicts)
Noel Edmonds has made headlines for plotting to buy the BBC, starting a pet counselling service, and driving a mannequin called Candice around in his black cab to dissuade the public from trying to flag him down.

Ted Rogers ➤ (3-2-1)
Terry Wogan ➤ (Blankety Blank)
Les Dawson ➤ (Blankety Blank)
Larry Grayson ➤ (The Generation Game)

Popular Food in the 1980s

Our last trolley dash takes us down the aisle at lunchtime, piled high with eat-on-the-go snacks and sandwiches. Stop on the way home for a deep pan pizza and a Diet Coke; end the day with a slice of Battenberg cake. Congratulations, you've just eaten the eighties!

Crunchy Nut Cornflakes
The cereal was invented in Manchester in 1980. Pity the poor Americans: it took 30 years for Crunchy Nut to cross the Atlantic.

Kellogg's Fruit and Fibre

Prepacked sandwiches
The prepacked sandwich was first sold by M&S in spring 1980. The range was small, conservative, made in-store and used whatever ingredients were plentiful (even if that was pilchards).

Viennetta

Trifle
In 1596, Thomas Dawson recorded the first recipe for trifle in his books, *The Good Huswifes Jewell*. It was essentially thick cream, rosewater, sugar and ginger. Jelly didn't appear until the 1700s.

Chicken Kiev

Vol au vent

Battenberg cake

Pizza
Pizza Hut claim to be the first company to sell food online – one of their signature pizzas via their Pizanet website, back in 1994.

Garlic bread

Kiwi

Sun-dried tomatoes

Potato waffles

Happy Meals

Diet Coke
Within two years of its unveiling in 1982, Diet Coke became the most popular diet soft drink in the world, and the third most popular soft drink overall behind Coca Cola and Pepsi.

Rowntree's Drifters

Hedgehog-flavoured crisps

Burton's fish 'n' chips

Chicken satay

Eighties Symbols of Success

In the flamboyant era of Dallas and Dynasty there were many ways to show that you, too, had really made it. Forty years on, it's fascinating to see how some of these throwbacks are outdated or available to nearly everyone, while others are still reserved for today's wealthy peacocks.

Car phone
Dishwasher
Children at private school
Waterbed
The modern-day waterbed was designed by a US student for his master's thesis project. Original fillings included corn syrup, and then jelly, before he settled on water. They were popular but problematic due to their weight and susceptibility to puncture, as Edward Scissorhands found out.

Second cars
Holidays abroad
Conservatory
Pony
Colour TV
Diamonds
Cordless phone
Birkin bag
A chance encounter between Hermès Executive Chairman Jean-Louis Dumas and Jane Birkin on a plane inspired the Birkin bag. The contents of Birkin's bag spilled out, and Dumas suggested she needed a bag with pockets, so Birkin sketched her idea on a sick bag.

Double glazing
Rolex watch
Leather Filofax
Mont Blanc pen
Newton's Cradle desk toy
Named after Isaac Newton and the cat's cradle, an early version was wooden, expensive and sold at Harrods. Chrome imitations followed. TV programme Myth Busters built a supersized cradle with concrete-filled chrome wrecking balls... it didn't work.

Stone cladding

Mary Evans/Classic Stock/J Nettis

The first UK car phone call was made in 1959 from outside the Lymm Hotel in Cheshire; human operators were used to connect calls until the 1980s. John Lennon wrote the lyrics for I'm Only Sleeping on the back of a car phone demand letter.

Cars of the 1980s

Many cars you might associate with the eighties were on the road long before then, from the Ford Granada and Escort to the Porsche 911. But this is the decade they arguably hit their stride alongside other automotive icons.

Toyota Corolla
Introduced in 1966, the Toyota Corolla became the best-selling car worldwide by 1974. The car was named after a ring of petals.

Volvo 240

BMW 3 Series

Volkswagen Golf
Sold as the Rabbit in the US and the Caribe in Mexico.

Volkswagen Passat

Vauxhall Astra

Triumph Acclaim

Porsche 911
Originally the Porsche 901 on its 1964 debut, the name was changed after Peugeot claimed they had exclusive rights to naming cars with three digits and a zero in the middle.

Jaguar XJS

Nissan Micra

Peugeot 205

Austin Maestro

Vauxhall Nova
The Vauxhall Nova inspired a series of comical bumper stickers, including 'You've been Novataken', and 'Vauxhall Casanova'. It was called the Corsa everywhere but Britain where it sounded too much like the word 'coarser'. It was renamed anyway in 1993.

Ford Sierra
Neil Kinnock had one of the first Sierras. He wrecked it in a crash.

Austin Montego

Volkswagen Polo

Austin Metro
Promoted with comical adverts, the car became one of the best-selling cars in UK history, and even Princess Diana owned one.

Ford Fiesta
The Fiesta is the UK's best-selling car of all time.

Vauxhall Cavalier

Eighties TV Gameshows

By the eighties, new formats aimed at youngsters – your youngsters? – were introduced. Some shows went digital or took to the skies; others kept it (very) simple, and a few remain family favourites to this day.

The Adventure Game

Treasure Hunt

Blind Date

The pilot episode of Blind Date was hosted by Duncan Norvelle, but he was quickly replaced by Cilla Black. Black presented the entire original run of the series for eighteen years, before unexpectedly announcing her departure on the show's first ever live episode.

Surprise Surprise

Countdown

Catchphrase

Blockbusters

Telly Addicts

3-2-1

The show's mascot and booby prize, Dusty Bin, cost around £10,000 to build. He was built by visual effects engineer Ian Rowley, who also operated Dusty Bin in the studio.

Blankety Blank

Bob's Full House

The instantly recognisable scoreboard was dubbed Mr Babbage by original host Bob Monkhouse. This was a nod to Charles Babbage, the inventor of the first programmable computer. In the reboot, Mr Babbage was replaced with a colour scoreboard, but the original board soon returned.

Bullseye

Cheggers Plays Pop

Family Fortunes

The Great Egg Race

Give Us a Clue

The Krypton Factor

Play Your Cards Right

The Price is Right

The Pyramid Game

Popular Girls' Names

Of the fifty names that made the Top 10 from 1900-74, only four have appeared since: Claire, Emma, Samantha and Sarah. (Oddly, names beginning with 'D' are now a rarity with no Top 10 entries in the last fifty years!)

Chloe
This is the third of six years on top for Chloe.

Emily

Megan
Chloe, Emily, Megan: for four years from 1998 to 2001, these were locked in as the top three choices for UK parents.

Olivia
Sophie
Charlotte
Lauren
Jessica
Rebecca
Hannah
Bethany
Georgia
Lucy
Amy
Katie
Ellie
Emma
Courtney
Eleanor
Abigail
Shannon
Molly
Holly
Jade
Caitlin
Alice

Rising and falling stars:
Eve, Charlie and Cerys: welcome to the Top 100!
Ashleigh and Sian: we're afraid your time is up.

Books of the Decade

Our final decade of books are the bookstore favourites from your fifties. How many did you read…and can you remember the plot, or the cover?

1989	A Prayer for Owen Meany by John Irving
1989	The Remains of the Day by Kazuo Ishiguro
1990	Possession by AS Byatt
1990	The Buddha of Suburbia by Hanif Kureishi
1991	Regeneration by Pat Barker
1991	**American Psycho by Bret Easton Ellis** Ellis received death threats before the book was published on account of the violent and misogynistic content. He had to indemnify his publisher from being sued by his family if he were murdered.
1992	The Secret History by Donna Tartt
1992	All the Pretty Horses by Cormac McCarthy
1992	The English Patient by Michael Ondaatje
1993	The Shipping News by E Annie Proulx
1993	Birdsong by Sebastian Faulks
1994	A Suitable Boy by Vikram Seth
1995	A Fine Balance by Rohinton Mistry
1996	Infinite Jest by David Foster Wallace
1996	**A Game of Thrones by George RR Martin** The idea for the story came to Martin as a child through his pet turtles. They lived in a toy castle, and he pretended they were kings, lords and knights, and imagined that they died because they killed each other battling for the castle.
1996	Bridget Jones's Diary by Helen Fielding
1997	**Harry Potter And The Philosopher's Stone by J K Rowling** In the film of the book, the late Rik Mayall played the part of Peeves the Poltergeist. The scene was cut before release.
1997	American Pastoral by Philip Roth
1997	The God of Small Things by Arundhati Roy
1997	Underworld by Don DeLillo
1997	Blindness by José Saramago
1998	The Poisonwood Bible by Barbara Kingsolver

April 17 1970: Jim Lovell is brought aboard a helicopter, the last of the
three astronauts from the Apollo 13 mission to be lifted from the floating

Apollo Astronauts

Not all of those who have been to the moon are equally well known. Twelve landed; twelve remained in orbit. Gus Grissom, Ed White, and Roger B Chaffee died in training. BBC and ITV broadcast the Apollo 11 landing live, in the first all-night transmission. The landing was at 9.17pm, but Armstrong didn't take one monumental step until 3.56am.

Landed on the moon:

Alan Bean

Alan Shepard

Shepard was the oldest person to walk on the moon at the age of 47.

Buzz Aldrin

Charles Duke

David Scott

Edgar Mitchell

Eugene Cernan

Harrison Schmitt

James Irwin

John Young

Neil Armstrong

Pete Conrad

Remained in low orbit:

Al Worden

Bill Anders

Anders took the iconic Earthrise photo.

Dick Gordon

Frank Borman

Fred Haise

Jack Swigert

Jim Lovell

Ken Mattingly

Michael Collins

Ron Evans

Made the final spacewalk of the program to retrieve film cassettes.

Stuart Roosa

On the Apollo 14 mission he carried seeds from 5 species of trees. They were planted across the US and are known as Moon Trees.

Tom Stafford

NASA

Popular Boys' Names

60

The most favoured names are now a curious blend of the evergreen (Thomas), the rediscovered (Harry), and those enjoying their first proper outing (Joshua).

Jack
This is Jack's fourth year on top. He'll remain the nation's first choice from 1996 to 2008.

Thomas
James
Joshua
Daniel
Matthew
Samuel
Joseph
Callum
William
Ryan
Luke
Lewis
Harry
Benjamin
Jordan
Liam
George
Oliver
Alexander
Adam
Connor
Jake
Cameron
Nathan
Michael

Rising and falling stars:
While names fell in and out of fashion in great numbers in the seventies and eighties, the pace has slowed. New this year: Ewan, Oscar, Taylor, Mason and Lucas. Out: longstanding stalwarts Steven, Paul and Richard.

Things People Did When You Were Growing Up (Part 2)

Finally, here are more of the things we saw, we did and errands we ran as kids that nobody needs, wants, or even understands how to do in the modern age!

+ Drink syrup of figs
+ Preserve vegetables
+ Save the silver chocolate papers from Roses
+ **Eat offal**
  Tripe was never on ration but long out of favour by the time the tripe dresser's fate was sealed in 1992, when BSE broke out.

+ **Make a carbon copy**
  Carbon paper was first patented by Ralph Wedgwood, son of Thomas Wedgwood, in 1806, for his Noctograph – designed to help blind people write without ink. The smell and texture are just a memory, but emails sent in 'cc' (carbon copy) might remind you!

+ **Wash handkerchiefs**
  You'd have to keep (and wash) a hanky for nine years to outweigh the CO_2 emissions of its tissue cousins.

+ Use talcum powder
+ Make a penfriend
+ **Wire a plug**
  Strip and route wires to the terminal; fit the right fuse. Not any more. In 1994, it became illegal to sell appliances without fitted plugs.

+ Darn a hole in your sock
+ Refill your pen from an inkwell
+ Wind on your camera for another shot
+ See the bones in your foot at the shoe shop through a Pedoscope
+ Pluck a chicken
+ **Smoke on a bus**
  'When will this fanaticism going to stop?' asked one MP in 1962, about a proposed ban on lower-deck smoking.

+ Scrape ice patterns off the inside of your bedroom window
+ Service your own car
+ Buy starch or blue bags for your washing
+ **Play Spot the Ball**
  Spot the Ball was launched in 1973. More than 10 years passed without a jackpot winner as its popularity declined.

The Biggest Hits When You Were 60

We're not reaching back very far for these hits - but unless you're very young at heart, that probably means you won't know very many of them!

Chocolate Salty Balls ♪ Chef

Heartbeat ♪ Steps

Praise You ♪ Fatboy Slim
The Praise You music video was directed by Spike Jonze - who also directed films such as Being John Malkovich. He is also the man seen dancing in the footage in a guerrilla music video that cost less than $1,000 to make.

Fly Away ♪ Lenny Kravitz

Baby One More Time ♪ Britney Spears
Britney Spears was only 16 years old when she released this career-defining pop track.

When the Going Gets Tough ♪ Boyzone

I Want It That Way ♪ Backstreet Boys

Sweet Like Chocolate ♪ Shanks and Bigfoot

Sunscreen ♪ Baz Luhrmann
The lyrics to the song are an essay titled, 'Advice, like youth, probably just wasted on the young' that originally appeared as a newspaper column.

Boom Boom Boom Boom ♪ Vengaboys

Livin' la Vida Loca ♪ Ricky Martin

Mambo No.5 ♪ Lou Bega
Mambo No.5 - an adaptation of a 1949 Cuban hit - also had chart success when it was covered by children's television character Bob the Builder.

The Millennium Prayer ♪ Cliff Richard

Printed in Great Britain
by Amazon

72501903R00066